HOOKED ON LIBRARY SKILLS!

A Sequential Activities Program for Grades K-6

**Marguerite Lewis
and
Pamela J. Kudla**

**THE CENTER FOR APPLIED
RESEARCH IN EDUCATION**
West Nyack, New York 10995

Library of Congress Catalog Card No.: 87-043341

Printed in the United States of America
20 19 18 17 16 15 14 13 12 11

ISBN 0-87628-408-X

**THE CENTER FOR APPLIED RESEARCH
IN EDUCATION**
West Nyack, NY 10994

On the World Wide Web at http://www.phdirect.com

This resource is dedicated to Dick in appreciation of his understanding and encouragement.

ABOUT THE AUTHORS

MARGUERITE LEWIS has been a Library Media Specialist in the Bethlehem Central School District, Delmar, New York, since 1969. She received her Bachelor of Science degree from Boston University and her Master's Degree in Educational Communications from the State University of New York at Albany.

Mrs. Lewis has published articles, activities, and puzzles in professional and children's magazines. She is also the creator of *Library Bingo* and the co-creator with Pamela J. Lewis Kudla of *Library Curriculum Flashcards,* both published in 1980 by Larlin Corporation, Marietta, Georgia. Mrs. Lewis also teamed with Pamela Kudla to write *Hooked on Research! Ready-to-Use Projects and Crosswords for Practice in Basic Library Skills* (The Center for Applied Research in Education, 1984) and *Hooked on Reading! 114 Wordsearch and Crossword Puzzles Based on the Newbery and Caldecott Award Winners* (The Center for Applied Research in Education, 1986). A book reviewer for *School Library Journal,* Mrs. Lewis is currently assigned to the Glenmont Elementary School in the Bethlehem Central School District.

PAMELA J. KUDLA received her Bachelor's Degree in Graphic Design from Rochester Institute of Technology, Rochester, New York. She was design consultant for *New York Alive* magazine, as well as assistant art director for Communication and Design, an advertising agency in Latham, New York, and an art director for B. Sterling Benkhart, Ltd., an advertising and photography studio in Newport, Rhode Island. Mrs. Kudla is currently working on freelance projects.

ABOUT *HOOKED ON LIBRARY SKILLS!*

Students today need to develop the ability to retrieve and interpret information, and must begin in the elementary grades to master the skills and techniques necessary to achieve success. These skills and techniques must be taught in a comprehensive and sequential curriculum beginning in kindergarten, and *Hooked on Library Skills! A Sequential Activities Program for Grades K-6* has been written for exactly this purpose.

Hooked on Library Skills! provides 40 lessons, one for each week of the school year, for grades K-6. Full-page activity sheets that can be reproduced as many times as needed are included with many of the lessons. This book makes it possible for you and classroom teachers—as a team—to plan, teach, review, and reinforce information skills and literature appreciation. After you introduce the students to a particular lesson, the classroom teacher will be able to integrate the skills into the academic curriculum.

The library skills and techniques taught in this book include:

Kindergarten

- caring for and handling materials
- listening to a story
- returning books to the proper place in the library

Grade 1

- knowing the different areas of the library
- understanding the sign-out procedure
- understanding alphabetizing and the call number

Grade 2

- reviewing the parts of a book
- understanding the difference between fiction and nonfiction
- appreciating literature and illustrations (through Caldecott Award winners)

Grade 3

- working with the card catalog

- preparing a brief biographical report
- using an encyclopedia and an atlas

Grade 4

- understanding the Dewey Decimal Classification System
- working with various reference books
- understanding cross references

Grade 5

- reading Newbery Award-winning books
- outlining and paraphrasing
- using the vertical file

Grade 6

- preparing a book report
- locating and interpreting information
- using the *Readers' Guide to Periodical Literature*

The lessons in *Hooked on Library Skills!* are flexible. If your school year begins in the middle of August, for example, simply begin with the first lesson and continue for four-week units, adjusting the seasonal literature. The timing of the units can be changed, too, to correspond with the academic curriculum. For instance, if a fifth or sixth grade teacher plans to begin the year with a research paper, start with that unit.

Hooked on Library Skills! is designed to be used with the individual school's own book collection. With over 2,000 children's books published annually, collections vary. Acquisitions are determined by budget, academic curriculum, and in-house needs and interests. The collection may not include a particular title but have another title on the same subject or genre of equal value. An activity based on a certain title is of no use if the title is unavailable, and a lesson planned around a particular title is of only partial value if there are multiple classes on that grade level. A title used with a class should circulate within that class for as long as requests continue.

Therefore, all of the *Hooked on Library Skills!* lessons can be utilized through the available collection. The skills, the objectives, the literature, the preparation, and the lesson can be followed regardless of the size of your collection or the number of sections of a grade housed in the school. We hope you and your students will enjoy using these activities!

Marguerite Lewis
Pamela J. Kudla

CONTENTS

Activity Sheets

Choose the Term
Choose the Concept

Activity Sheet

How Books Are Shelved

Activity Sheets

Fiction—Nonfiction
Shelving Fiction and Nonfiction Books

April • 104

Activity Sheets

Map of the United States
My Favorite Tall Tale Character

May • 109

June • 110

Activity Sheets

Magazines
My Favorite Magazine

GRADE 3 **115**

Overview • 115

September • 117

Activity Sheets

Treasure Hunt in _____
The Business of Books
What Part of the Book Am I?
It's All Part of the Story

Activity Sheets

Outline for Biography Hornbook
Biography Hornbook

Activity Sheets

Selecting the Right Volume
Guide Words
Using Key Words

Activity Sheet

Atlas Practice

Activity Sheets

State Slips
United States Project

Activity Sheets

Card Catalog Puzzle
Book Terms Scramble
A Bouquet of Facts
Authors and Characters

Activity Sheets

Newbery Gold Medal Winners
Newbery Award Books I've Read
The Newbery Story
Parts of the Book
Concepts and Parts of the Story

Activity Sheets

Practice Using a Gazetteer or Geographical Dictionary
Biographical Dictionaries
Practice Using Author Reference Books
The Vertical File

Activity Sheets

Comparison of Information in Encyclopedias #1
Comparison of Information in Encyclopedias #2
Comparison of Information in Encyclopedias—An Opinion Poll

Contents

Contents

KINDERGARTEN

OVERVIEW

The main objectives in kindergarten are:

- to create an atmosphere through which the students will regard the library as a warm, inviting, friendly, interesting place to visit.
- to help the students develop listening and discussion skills.
- to teach the students the proper care of books.
- to help the students begin to develop an appreciation of literature.
- to introduce, review, and reinforce library terms and concepts.

Terms and Concepts

Browsing	Dust Jacket	Overhead Projector
Turning Pages	Library/media center	Transparency
Care of Books	Librarian	Computer
Author	Media Specialist	Disk
Title	Filmstrip Projector	Hardware
Spine	Filmstrip	Software
Cover	Record Player/Phonograph	Circulation Desk
Pages	Record	Workroom
Illustrator	Cassette Player/Recorder	
Illustrations	Cassette	

Literature Genre

ABC Books	Dogs—Puppies	Adults	Airplanes
Counting Books	Family	Children	Automobiles
Mother Goose	Horses	Birds	Libraries
Halloween	Elephants	Ducks	Books in a series
Mice	Giraffes	Spring	Seasonal
Bears	Alligators	Boats	Summer
Cats—Kittens	Birthdays	Trains	

Attendance

Taking attendance adds importance to the class. It helps the librarian learn the names of the students, and it provides a record for the librarian.

Special Words for Attendance

Having students use special words—such as "black," "orange," "apple," "banana"—for attendance and for returning books is a thinking skill. It is also an incentive to return books on time. If a student is asked why he or she does not borrow books, the response is always that there are no books. It also helps the librarian to know how many students will be borrowing books each day, to gauge the time needed for book selection. It keeps a good check on the students' borrowing habits.

Story Candle

Listening to a story is a skill. Creating an atmosphere conducive to listening is an aid in encouraging the development of this skill. Plugging in a small single candle—the type used in windows during holiday time—helps the students to understand that this is a quiet, listening time.

Story Bag Tales

The Story Bag helps students retain knowledge of stories read. The students feel they are participating in the planning of the lesson. The students choose the object, the librarian selects the story. The Story Bag activity will take as many weeks as there are students in the class.

SEPTEMBER

Lesson 1

SKILL: Listening to a story, group discussion, turning pages.

OBJECTIVE: Students will begin to understand and accept proper library behavior. Students will browse through books, turning pages properly.

PREPARATION: Roster of students in attendance book. Book to read to class. Selection of books on tables. Story candle.

LESSON: Students meet in story corner. Check attendance. Discuss briefly "the library." Read and discuss story. Move to tables. Demonstrate the proper procedure for turning pages. Have students browse through books.

DISMISSAL: Students return to story corner. Review lesson. Dismiss.

Lesson 2

SKILL: Care of books.

OBJECTIVE: Students will be introduced to the proper care of books.

PREPARATION: Filmstrip or other media on the care of books. Selection of books on tables. Story candle (as story candle will be used each week, it will not be included with preparation).

LESSON: Students meet in story corner. Check attendance. Review last week's story. Introduce care of books. Show filmstrip, discuss. Have students move to tables and browse through books.

DISMISSAL: Students return to story corner. Review care of books. Students will begin to borrow books next week. Stress having a book bag to protect books. Dismiss.

Lesson 3

SKILL: Browsing and selecting a book.

OBJECTIVE: Students will browse through displayed books and select one.

PREPARATION: Display a selection of books on tables. Provide a bookmark for each student. Choose an author of many books. Choose one to read to class and show the others.

LESSON: Students meet in story corner. Check attendance. Review last week's story. Introduce author and show books. Introduce story, read, and discuss.

BOOK SELECTION: Students browse and select books. Have books signed out. Students will return to story corner and read books until all students have returned. Review care of books. Give each student a book mark. Dismiss.

Lesson 4

SKILL: Learning to take turns. Recall of story and characters.

OBJECTIVE: Begin Story Bag Tales. Students will begin to participate in lesson planning.

PREPARATION: Make a copy of the Story Bag check-off sheet. The Story Bag should be filled and ready. Display a selection of books on tables. Select a story or filmstrip to use with class.

LESSON: Students meet in story corner.
Check attendance. Orange—book returned
Brown—book not returned

Review last week's story. Introduce this week's story, read and introduce the Story Bag. Have a student reach into the Story Bag and withdraw an object. Explain next week's story will be about the object. Record student's name and object on check-off sheet. Tell briefly of books on display.

BOOK SELECTION: Students select books and return to story corner. Review lesson. Review next week's object. Dismiss.

STORY BAG CHARACTERS
Check-off Sheet

___ AIRPLANE

___ AUTOMOBILE

___ BEAR

___ BEAVER

___ BIRD

___ BIRTHDAY CAKE

___ BOAT

___ CAMEL

___ CANDY

___ CAT-KITTEN

___ CHICKEN

___ CROCODILE

___ DONKEY

___ DUCK

___ ELEPHANT

___ FISH

___ FROG

___ GIRAFFE

___ GHOST

___ GOOSE

___ HAT

___ HORSE

___ KANGAROO

___ MONKEY

___ PENGUIN

___ PURPLE CRAYON

___ RABBIT

___ REINDEER

___ ROOSTER

___ TIGER

___ TURTLE

STORY BAG PATTERN

FOLD

1. Cut one piece 15½ inches wide and 29 inches long.
2. Turn down top 3¼ inches. Stitch 1/4 inch hem.
3. Stitch one inch from hem to form drawstring facing.
4. Stitch sides to bottom circle, placing cardboard between circles for stability.
5. *Drawstring*: Bulky wool at least 38 inches long.

FOLD

STORY BAG PATTERN

Cut two circles from fabric, plus one circle of cardboard on dotted lines or 1/2 inch smaller than the outer circle. Stitch circle to sides, placing cardboard between circles.

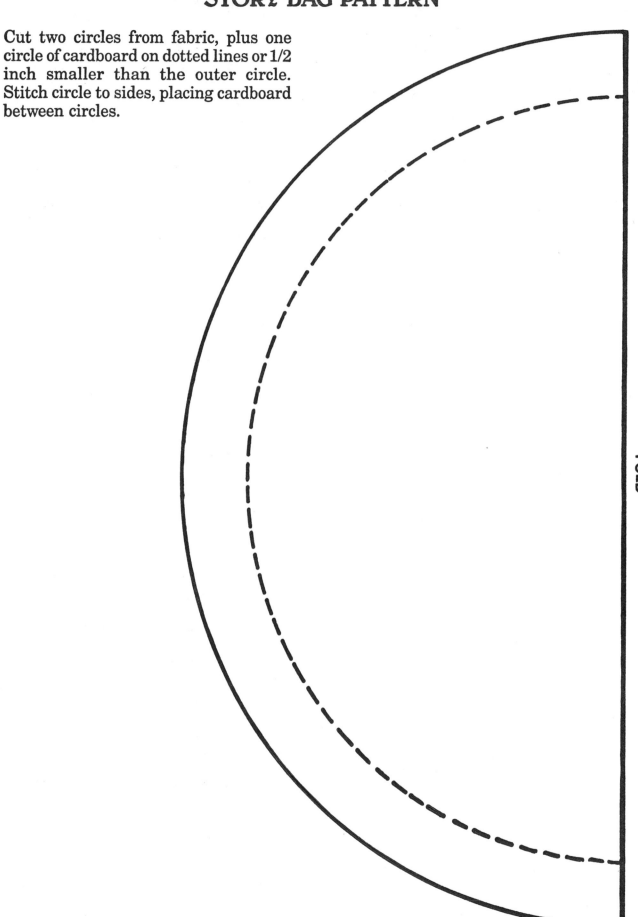

FOLD

STORY BAG CHARACTERS

CRAYON

STORY BAG CHARACTERS

Happy Birthday!

STORY BAG CHARACTERS

STORY BAG CHARACTERS

STORY BAG CHARACTERS

Class: _____

DATE	STUDENT	OBJECT	TITLE READ

OCTOBER

Lesson 1

SKILL: Students will review and reinforce the proper care of books.

OBJECTIVE: Students will return books on time. Students will begin to care for books properly.

ALTERNATE LITERATURE: ABC books

PREPARATION: Story Bag. Display books on the subject drawn from the Story Bag or alternate literature. Select one to use with class.

LESSON: Students meet in story corner.
Check attendance. Black—book returned
Orange—book not returned

Review and remove object from Story Bag. Introduce story, read, and discuss. Select object for next week. Record on chart. Student who selects object has first choice of borrowing book.

BOOK SELECTION: Students select books and return to story corner. Review lesson and next week's object. Dismiss.

Lesson 2

SKILL: Location of places in the library.

OBJECTIVE: Students will be introduced to appropriate areas of the library.

ALTERNATE LITERATURE: Counting books.

PREPARATION: Story Bag. Display books on object drawn from Story Bag or alternate literature. Select one to use with class.

LESSON: Meet in story corner.
Check attendance. Black—book returned
Orange—book not returned

Review and remove objects from Story Bag. Introduce this week's object and story, read and discuss. Select object for next week and record on chart. Walk the students around the library pointing out areas of interest to them.

BOOK SELECTION: Students return to story corner after selecting books. Review story and lesson. Dismiss.

Lesson 3

SKILL: Proper placement of returned library books.

OBJECTIVE: Students will return their books to the proper place.

ALTERNATE LITERATURE: Mother Goose rhymes.

PREPARATION: Story Bag. Display books on object drawn from Story Bag or alternate literature. Select one to use with the class.

LESSON: Meet students at the door. Demonstrate the proper placement of library books. Have students place books properly.
Meet in story corner.
Check attendance. Black—book returned
                                    Orange—book not returned

Review and remove Story Bag objects. Introduce this week's object and story, read and discuss. Select object for next week. Record on chart. Tell briefly of books on display.

BOOK SELECTION: Students return to story corner after selecting book. Review lesson. Review placement of books. Dismiss.

Lesson 4

SKILL: Returning books to proper place in library.

OBJECTIVE: All students will return their books to the proper place in the library.

ALTERNATE LITERATURE: Halloween fiction and nonfiction.

PREPARATION: Story Bag. Display books on object drawn from Story Bag or alternate literature. Select one to use with class.

LESSON: Meet class at the door. Have class place books properly, then go to story corner, without assistance. Discuss results.
Check attendance. Black—book returned
                                    Orange—book not returned

Review and remove objects from Story Bag. Introduce this week's story, read and discuss. Select for next week. Record on chart.

BOOK SELECTION: Students return to story corner. Review story and lesson. Dismiss.

NOVEMBER

Lesson 1

SKILL: Concept of author.

OBJECTIVE: Students will become familiar with the term "author."

ALTERNATE LITERATURE: Mice—fiction and nonfiction.

PREPARATION: Chalkboard or display board. Make a sign of the word author. Story Bag. Display books on object drawn from Story Bag or alternate literature. Select one to use with the class.

LESSON: Meet in story corner.
Check attendance. Yellow—book returned
Blue—book not returned

Using the sign, introduce the concept of author. Review and remove Story Bag objects. Introduce this week's story, read, and discuss. Select object for next week. Record on chart.

BOOK SELECTION: Students return to story corner. Review author. Point out author on student's books. Review story and object. Dismiss.

Lesson 2

SKILL: Concept of author and title.

OBJECTIVE: Students will review the concept of author and will become familiar with the term "title."

ALTERNATE LITERATURE: Bears—fiction and nonfiction.

PREPARATION: Chalkboard or display board. Copy of words author and title. Story Bag. Display books on object drawn from Story Bag or alternate literature. Select one to use with the class.

LESSON: Meet in story corner.
Check attendance. Yellow—book returned
Blue—book not returned

Using the signs, review author, and introduce title. Review and remove objects drawn from Story Bag. Introduce this week's story, read, and discuss. Tell briefly of books on display.

> *BOOK SELECTION:* Students return to story corner. Review author and title. Point out author and title on students books. Review story and object. Dismiss.

Lesson 3

SKILL: Concept of author and title. Parts of the book: spine and cover.

OBJECTIVE: Students will review and reinforce the concept of author and title. Students will be introduced to the spine and cover.

ALTERNATE LITERATURE: Cats and kittens—fiction and nonfiction.

PREPARATION: Chalkboard or display board. A copy of the phrase, 'parts of the book' and a copy of the words spine and cover. A copy of the words author and title. Display books on the subject drawn from the Story Bag or alternate literature. Select one to use with the class.

> *LESSON:* Meet in story corner.
> Check attendance. Yellow—book returned
> Blue—book not returned
>
> Review author and title. Introduce the parts of the book and spine and cover. Review and remove objects from Story Bag. Introduce story, read, and discuss. Select for next week. Record on chart. Tell briefly of books on display.
>
> *BOOK SELECTION:* Students return to story corner. Review concepts. Review lesson. Dismiss.

Lesson 4

SKILL: Parts of the book: spine, cover, and pages.

OBJECTIVE: Students will review and reinforce the spine and cover. Students will be introduced to the pages.

ALTERNATE LITERATURE: Dogs and puppies—fiction and nonfiction.

PREPARATION: Chalkboard or display board. Story Bag. A copy of the words author, title, spine, and cover. A copy of the word pages. Display books on object drawn from story bag or alternate literature. Select one to use with class.

> *LESSON:* Meet in story corner.
> Check attendance. Yellow—book returned
> Blue—book not returned

Review author, title, spine, and cover. Introduce pages. Review and remove objects from Story Bag. Introduce this week's story, read, and discuss. Select for next week. Record on chart. Tell briefly of books on display.

BOOK SELECTION: Students return to story corner. Review lesson. Review object for next week. Dismiss.

DECEMBER

Lesson 1

SKILL: Concept of author, title, and illustrator.

OBJECTIVE: Students will review and reinforce author and title. Students will be introduced to illustrator.

ALTERNATE LITERATURE: Family fiction and nonfiction.

PREPARATION: Chalkboard or display board. A copy of author and title. Make a copy of illustrator. Story Bag. Display books on object drawn from Story Bag or alternate literature. Select one to use with the class.

LESSON: Meet in story corner.
    Check attendance. Red—book returned
                    Green—book not returned

Review author and title. Introduce illustrator. Review and remove objects drawn from Story Bag. Introduce story, read, and discuss. Select object for next week. Record on chart.

BOOK SELECTION: Students return to story corner. Review lesson. Review object for next week. Dismiss.

Lesson 2

SKILL: Concept of author, title, and illustrator.

OBJECTIVE: Students will review and reinforce concept of author, title, and illustrator.

ALTERNATE LITERATURE: Family and seasonal fiction and nonfiction.

PREPARATION: Chalkboard or display board. A copy of the words author, title, and illustrator. Story Bag. Display books on object drawn from Story Bag or alternate literature. Select one to use with class.

> *LESSON:* Meet in story corner.
> Check attendance. Red—book returned
> Green—book not returned
>
> Review author, title, and illustrator. Review and remove objects from Story Bag. Introduce this week's story, read, and discuss. Select object for next week. Record on chart. Tell briefly of books on display.
>
> *BOOK SELECTION:* Students return to story corner. Review lesson. Review object for next week. Dismiss.

Lesson 3

SKILL: Concept of author, title, illustrator, and illustrations.

OBJECTIVE: Students will review and reinforce author, title, and illustrator. Students will be introduced to the concept of illustrations.

ALTERNATE LITERATURE: Family and seasonal fiction and nonfiction.

PREPARATION: Chalkboard or display board. A copy of author, title, and illustrator. Make a copy of illustrations. Story Bag. Display books on object from Story Bag or alternate literature. Select one to use with the class.

> *LESSON:* Meet in story corner.
> Check attendance. Red—book returned
> Green—book not returned
>
> Review author, title, and illustrator. Introduce illustrations. Review and remove objects from Story Bag. Introduce, read, and discuss story. Select object for next week. Record on chart. Tell briefly of books on display.
>
> *BOOK SELECTION:* Students return to story corner. Review lesson. Review object for next week. Dismiss.

Lesson 4

SKILL: Concept of author, title, illustrator, and illustrations.

OBJECTIVE: Students will review and reinforce author, title, illustrator, and illustrations.

ALTERNATE LITERATURE: Family and seasonal fiction and nonfiction.

PREPARATION: Chalkboard or display board. A copy of author, title, illustrator, and illustrations. Story Bag. Display books on object from Story Bag or alternate literature. Select one to use with the class.

LESSON: Meet in story corner.
Check attendance. Red—book returned
Green—book not returned

Review author, title, illustrator, and illustrations. Review and remove objects from Story Bag. Introduce this week's story, read and discuss. Select object for next week. Record on chart.

BOOK SELECTION: Students return to story corner. Review lesson. Review object for next week. Dismiss.

JANUARY

Lesson 1

SKILL: Parts of the book: spine, cover, pages, and dust jacket.

OBJECTIVE: Students will review spine, cover, and pages. Students will be introduced to dust jacket.

ALTERNATE LITERATURE: Horses—fiction and nonfiction.

PREPARATION: Chalkboard or display board. A copy of spine, cover, pages, and dust jacket. Story Bag. Display books on object from Story Bag or alternate literature. Select one to use with class.

LESSON: Meet in story corner.
Check attendance. Gold—book returned
Silver—book not returned

Review spine, cover, and pages. Introduce dust jacket. Review and remove objects from Story Bag. Introduce this week's story, read, and discuss. Select object for next week. Record on chart. Tell briefly of books on display.

BOOK SELECTION: Students return to story corner. Review lesson. Review object for next week. Dismiss.

Lesson 2

SKILL: Parts of the book: spine, cover, pages, and dust jacket.

OBJECTIVE: Students will complete an activity designed to review spine, cover, pages, and dust jacket.

ALTERNATE LITERATURE: Elephants—fiction and nonfiction.

PREPARATION: Student copies of activity "Parts of the Book." Student crayons. A transparency of activity. Overhead projector. Story Bag. Display books on object from Story Bag or alternate literature. Select one to use with the class.

LESSON: Meet in story corner.
Check attendance. Gold—book returned
Silver—book not returned

Move to tables. Hand out activity and crayons. Introduce activity. Have students complete activity. If there is time, return to story corner and continue lesson with Story Bag.

BOOK SELECTION: Students return to story corner. Review lesson. Activity will go home with students. Dismiss.

Lesson 3

SKILL: Concepts of the book: author, title, illustrator, and illustrations.

OBJECTIVE: Students will review author, title, illustrator, and illustrations.

ALTERNATE LITERATURE: Giraffes—fiction and nonfiction.

PREPARATION: Chalkboard or display board. A copy of words author, title, illustrator, and illustrations. Story Bag. Display books from object from Story Bag or alternate literature. Select one to use with the class.

LESSON: Meet in story corner.
Check attendance. Gold—book returned
Silver—book not returned

Review author, title, illustrator, and illustrations. Review and remove Story Bag objects. Introduce this week's story, read, discuss. Select object for next week. Record on chart. Tell briefly of books on display.

BOOK SELECTION: Students return to story corner. Review lesson. Review for next week. Dismiss.

Lesson 4

SKILL: Concept of author, title, illustrator, and illustrations.

OBJECTIVE: Students will complete an activity designed to review author, title, illustrator, and illustrations.

ALTERNATE LITERATURE: Alligators/crocodiles—fiction and nonfiction.

PREPARATION: Student copies of activity "Book Words." Student crayons. A transparency of activity. Overhead projector. Display books on object from Story Bag or alternate literature. Select one to use with the class.

LESSON: Meet in story corner.
Check attendance. Gold—book returned
Silver—book not returned

Move to tables. Hand out activity and crayons. Introduce activity. Have students complete activity. If time, return to story corner and continue lesson with Story Bag.

BOOK SELECTION: Students return to story corner. Review lesson. Activity will go home with students. Dismiss.

PARTS OF THE BOOK

1. Find the word *Spine*. Color the letters *Orange*. 2. Find the word *Cover*. Color the letters *Purple*. 3. Find the word *Pages*. Color the letters *Brown*. 4. Find the word *Dust Jacket*. Color the letters *Black*.

Spine

Dust Jacket

Cover

Pages

Name —————

Date ——————

BOOK WORDS

1. Find the word *Author.* Color the letters *Red.* 2. Find the word *Title.* Color the letters *Blue.* 3. Find the word *Illustrator.* Color the letters *Green.* 4. Find the word *Illustrations.* Leave the letters *White.*

Title

Illustrations

ILLUSTRATOR

Author

FEBRUARY

Lesson 1

SKILL: Concept of filmstrip projector and filmstrip.

OBJECTIVE: Students will be introduced to the terms filmstrip projector and filmstrip.

ALTERNATE LITERATURE: Birthdays—fiction and nonfiction.

PREPARATION: Chalkboard or display board. A copy of the words filmstrip projector and filmstrip. Story Bag. Display books on object from Story Bag or alternate literature. Select a filmstrip version to use with the class.

LESSON: Meet in story corner.
　　　　　Check attendance. Grey—book returned
　　　　　　　　　　　　　　Pink—book not returned

Introduce and discuss filmstrip projector and filmstrip. Review and remove objects from Story Bag. Introduce this week's story, show and discuss. Select object for next week. Record on chart. Tell briefly of books on display.

BOOK SELECTION: Students return to story corner. Review lesson. Dismiss.

Lesson 2

SKILL: Concept of phonograph/record player and record.

OBJECTIVE: Students will be introduced to the terms phonograph/record player and record.

ALTERNATE LITERATURE: Adults—fiction and nonfiction.

PREPARATION: Chalkboard or display board. A copy of the words phonograph/record player and record. Story Bag. Display books on object from Story Bag or alternate literature. Select a record version to use with the class.

LESSON: Meet in story corner.
　　　　　Check attendance. Grey—book returned
　　　　　　　　　　　　　　Pink—book not returned

Introduce and discuss phonograph/record player and record. Review and remove objects from Story Bag. Introduce this week's record, play, and discuss. Select object for next week. Record on chart.

BOOK SELECTION: Students return to story corner. Review lesson. Dismiss.

Lesson 3

SKILL: Recognition of the terms filmstrip projector, filmstrip, phonograph/record player, and record.

OBJECTIVE: Students will recognize the terms and match up the hardware to the software.

ALTERNATE LITERATURE: Children—fiction and nonfiction.

PREPARATION: Chalkboard or display board. A copy of the terms. Story Bag. Display books on object from Story Bag or alternate literature. Select one to use with the class.

LESSON: Meet in story corner.
Check attendance. Grey—book returned
Pink—book not returned

Using terms, have students match up software to hardware. Review and remove objects from Story Bag. Introduce this week's story, read, and discuss. Select object for next week. Record on chart. Tell briefly of books on display.

BOOK SELECTION: Students return to story corner. Review lesson. Dismiss.

Lesson 4

SKILL: Mastery of the terms used in lesson three.

OBJECTIVE: Students will master matching the software with the hardware.

ALTERNATE LITERATURE: Children—fiction and nonfiction.

PREPARATION: Chalkboard or display board. A copy of the terms. Story Bag. Display books on object from Story Board or alternate literature. Select one to use with the class.

LESSON: Meet in story corner.
Check attendance. Grey—book returned
Pink—book not returned

Display terms in mixed up order. Students practice for mastery. Review and remove objects from Story Bag. Introduce this week's story, read, discuss. Select for next week. Record on chart. Tell briefly of books on display.

BOOK SELECTION: Students return to story corner. Review lesson. Dismiss.

MARCH

Lesson 1

SKILL: Recognition of the terms cassette recorder/player and cassette.

OBJECTIVE: Students will be introduced to the terms cassette recorder/player and cassette.

ALTERNATE LITERATURE: Birds—fiction and nonfiction.

PREPARATION: Chalkboard or display board. A copy of the terms. Story Bag. Display books on object from Story Bag or alternate literature. Use a cassette version of one with the class.

LESSON: Meet in story corner.
          Check attendance. Cream—book returned
                      Bronze—book not returned

Introduce and discuss cassette recorder/player and cassette. Review and remove objects from Story Bag. Introduce this week's story, read and discuss. Select for next week. Record on chart. Tell briefly of books on display.

BOOK SELECTION: Students return to story corner. Review lesson. Dismiss.

Lesson 2

SKILL: Recognition of the terms overhead projector and transparency.

OBJECTIVE: Students will be introduced to the terms overhead projector and transparency.

ALTERNATE LITERATURE: Ducks—fiction and nonfiction.

PREPARATION: Chalkboard or display board. A copy of the terms. Story Bag. Display books on object from Story Bag or alternate literature. Use some sort of transparency version with class.

LESSON: Meet in story corner.
          Check attendance. Cream—book returned
                      Bronze—book not returned

Introduce and discuss overhead projector and transparency. Review and remove objects from Story Bag. Introduce this week's story, read, and discuss. Select for next week. Record on chart. Tell briefly of books on display.

BOOK SELECTION: Students return to story corner. Review lesson. Dismiss.

Lesson 3

SKILL: Recognition of hardware and software.

OBJECTIVE: Students will recognize the terms cassette recorder/player and cassette and overhead projector and transparency.

ALTERNATE LITERATURE: Geese—fiction and nonfiction.

PREPARATION: Chalkboard or display board. A copy of the terms. Story Bag. Display books on object from Story Bag or alternate literature. Select one to use with the class.

LESSON: Meet in story corner.
    Check attendance. Cream—book returned
        Bronze—book not returned

Display terms mixed up on display board. Have students match hardware to software. Review and remove objects from Story Bag. Introduce this week's story, read, and discuss. Select for next week. Record on chart. Tell briefly of books on display.

BOOK SELECTION: Students return to story corner. Review lesson. Dismiss.

Lesson 4

SKILL: Mastery of the terms covered.

OBJECTIVE: Students will master the terms for the hardware and software already introduced.

ALTERNATE LITERATURE: Spring—fiction and nonfiction.

PREPARATION: Chalkboard or display board. A copy of all terms. Story Bag. Display books on object from Story Bag or alternate literature. Select an AV version to use with class.

LESSON: Meet in story corner.
    Check attendance. Cream—book returned
        Bronze—book not returned

Display terms in mixed up order. Students practice for mastery. Review and remove objects from Story Bag. Introduce this week's story, read, discuss. Story Bag should be completed by now. Tell briefly of books on display.

BOOK SELECTION: Students return to story corner. Review lesson. Dismiss.

APRIL

Lesson 1

SKILL: Recognition of the terms *computer* and *disk.*

OBJECTIVE: Students will be introduced to the terms computer, and disk.

LITERATURE: Vehicles—trains fiction and nonfiction.

PREPARATION: Chalkboard or display board. A copy of the terms computer and disk. Display a selection of books about trains, fiction and nonfiction. Select one to use with the class.

LESSON: Meet in story corner.
Check attendance. Purple—book returned
Lime—book not returned

Introduce and discuss computer and disk. Introduce trains and this week's story. Read and discuss. Tell briefly of books on display.

BOOK SELECTION: Students return to story corner. Review lesson. Dismiss.

Lesson 2

SKILL: Knowledge and understanding of the terms *computer* and *disk.*

OBJECTIVE: Students will master the terms computer and disk.

LITERATURE: Vehicle—automobiles fiction and nonfiction.

PREPARATION: Chalkboard or display board. A copy of the terms. Display a selection of books about automobiles fiction and nonfiction. Select one to use with the class.

LESSON: Meet in story corner.
Check attendance. Purple—book returned
Lime—book not returned

Review and reinforce the terms. If possible have a computer and disk for demonstration. Introduce automobiles and this week's story. Read and discuss. Tell briefly of books on display.

BOOK SELECTION: Students return to story corner. Review lesson. Dismiss.

Lesson 3

SKILL: Knowledge and understanding of the terms *hardware* and *software*.

OBJECTIVE: Students will be introduced to the meaning of the terms *hardware* and *software*.

LITERATURE: Vehicles—boats, fiction and nonfiction.

PREPARATION: Chalkboard or display board. A copy of the terms. Display a selection of books about boats, fiction and nonfiction. Select one to use with the class.

LESSON: Meet in story corner.
　　　　Check attendance. Purple—book returned
　　　　　　　　　　Lime—book not returned

Introduce the terms hardware and software. Introduce boats and this week's story. Read and discuss. Tell briefly of books on display.

BOOK SELECTION: Students return to story corner. Review lesson. Dismiss.

Lesson 4

SKILL: Mastery of hardware and software.

OBJECTIVE: Students will master the meaning of the terms hardware and software.

LITERATURE: Vehicles—airplanes, fiction and nonfiction.

PREPARATION: Chalkboard or display board. A copy of all the terms. A copy of the terms hardware and software. Display a selection of books about airplanes, fiction and nonfiction. Select one to use with the class.

LESSON: Meet in story corner.
　　　　Check attendance. Purple—book returned
　　　　　　　　　　Lime—book not returned

Display the terms hardware and software. Hold up each term. Students decide whether each term is hardware or software. Then match up the hardware with the correct software. Introduce airplanes and this week's story. Read and discuss. Tell briefly of books on display.

BOOK SELECTION: Students return to story corner. Review lesson. Dismiss.

MAY

Lesson 1

SKILL: Knowledge and understanding of library/media center and librarian/media specialist.

OBJECTIVE: Students will be introduced to the concepts of library/media center and librarian/media specialist.

LITERATURE: Libraries—fiction and nonfiction.

PREPARATION: Chalkboard or display board. A copy of the terms. Display a selection of books about libraries, fiction and nonfiction. Select one or a filmstrip to use with the class.

LESSON: Meet in story corner.
    Check attendance. Beige—book returned
                        Coral—book not returned

Introduce and discuss terms. Introduce story or filmstrip, read or show and discuss. Tell briefly of books on display.

BOOK SELECTION: Students meet in story corner. Review lesson. Dismiss.

Lesson 2

SKILL: Knowledge and understanding of different types of libraries.

OBJECTIVE: Students will be introduced to various types of libraries.

LITERATURE: Libraries—fiction and nonfiction.

PREPARATION: Chalkboard or display board. A copy of the terms. Pictures of various types of libraries. Display a selection of books about libraries, fiction and nonfiction. Select one to use with the class.

LESSON: Meet in story corner.
    Check attendance. Beige—book returned
                        Coral—book not returned

Review and discuss the various types of libraries. Discuss activities that occur in libraries. Introduce story, read and discuss. Tell briefly of books on display.

BOOK SELECTION: Students return to story corner. Review lesson. Dismiss.

Lesson 3

SKILL: Knowledge and understanding of parts of the facility.

OBJECTIVE: Students will be introduced to the circulation desk.

LITERATURE: Humorous fiction.

PREPARATION: Chalkboard or display board. A copy of the term. Display a selection of humorous fiction. Select one to use with the class.

LESSON: Meet in story corner.
Check attendance. Beige—book returned
Coral—book not returned

Introduce and discuss circulation desk. Introduce this week's story, read and discuss. Tell briefly of books on display.

BOOK SELECTION: Students return to story corner. Review lesson. Dismiss.

Lesson 4

SKILL: Knowledge and understanding of parts of the facility.

OBJECTIVE: Students will be introduced to the workroom.

LITERATURE: Humorous nonfiction.

PREPARATION: Chalkboard or display board. A copy of the term. Display a selection of humorous nonfiction. Select one to use with the class.

LESSON: Meet in story corner.
Check attendance. Beige—book returned
Coral—book not returned

Introduce and discuss workroom. Introduce this week's story, read and discuss. Tell briefly of books on display.

BOOK SELECTION: Students return to story corner. Review lesson. Dismiss.

JUNE

Lesson 1

SKILL: Knowledge and understanding of the parts of the book: spine, cover, pages, and dust jacket.

OBJECTIVE: Students will review the parts of the book.

LITERATURE: Books in a series.

PREPARATION: Blackboard or display board. A copy of the terms used in previous lessons. Display a selection of books in a series by one author. Select one to use with the class.

LESSON: Meet in story corner.
    Check attendance. Ivory—book returned
        Lavender—book not returned

Review and reinforce the parts of the book. Introduce books in a series. Introduce, read, and discuss story. Tell briefly of books on display.

BOOK SELECTION: Students return to story corner. Review lesson. Dismiss.

Lesson 2

SKILL: Knowledge and understanding of author, title, illustrator, and illustrations.

OBJECTIVE: Students will review their knowledge of author, title, illustrator, and illustrations.

LITERATURE: Books in a series.

PREPARATION: Chalkboard or display board. A copy of the terms. Display a selection of books in a series. Select one to use with the class.

LESSON: Meet in story corner.
    Check attendance. Ivory—book returned
        Lavender—book not returned

Review and reinforce the terms. Introduce books in a series. Introduce, read, and discuss story. Tell briefly of books on display.

BOOK SELECTION: Students return to story corner. Review lesson. Dismiss.

Lesson 3

SKILL: Knowledge and understanding of hardware and software.

OBJECTIVE: Students will review and reinforce their knowledge of hardware and software.

LITERATURE: Summer—fiction and nonfiction.

PREPARATION: Chalkboard or display board. A copy of the terms of all the hardware and software covered during the year. Display a selection of books about summer, fiction and nonfiction. Select one to use with the class.

LESSON: Meet in story corner.
        Check attendance. Ivory—book returned
                  Lavender—book not returned

Review and reinforce the terms. Introduce story, read, and discuss. Tell briefly of books on display.

BOOK SELECTION: Students return to story corner. Review lesson. Dismiss.

Lesson 4

SKILL: Knowledge and understanding of the parts of the facility.

OBJECTIVE: Students will review and be introduced to various parts of the facility.

LITERATURE: As this is the last lesson, there probably will be no book selection.

PREPARATION: Chalkboard or display board. A copy of the terms. Select a story or filmstrip to use with the class.

LESSON: Meet in story corner.
        Check attendance. Ivory—book returned
                  Lavender—book not returned

Review the terms already covered and introduce any other areas that the students should know. Introduce story, read, and discuss. Review any other areas of the curriculum necessary. Discuss summer programs of interest to the students. Dismiss.

GRADE 1

OVERVIEW

The main objectives in first grade are:
- to begin the process that will lead to independent use of the library.
- to help the students master checkout procedures.
- to help the students understand the arrangement of materials.
- to build on the students knowledge and understanding of library and book terms and concepts.
- to introduce genres of literature and nonfiction to help the students begin to develop their own individual interest areas.

Terms, Concepts, and Skills

Review
Spine, Cover, Pages, Dust Jacket,
Author, Title, Illustrator, Illustrations

Filmstrip and Filmstrip Projector, Record and Record Player/Phonograph, Cassette and Cassette Player/Recorder, Transparency and Overhead Projector, Computer and Disk

Library/Media Center, Librarian/Media Specialist

New

Location of Materials	Call Number
Book Card, Book Pocket, Date Due Slip	Alphabetizing
Checkout Procedures	Fiction
Publisher	Nonfiction
Copyright	Characters
Copyright Date	Setting
Plot	Parts of a story

Attendance

Taking attendance adds importance to the class. It helps the librarian learn the students' names. It provides a record of absences. It provides a record of students' borrowing habits.

Special Words for Attendance

Using special words for attendance rather than "yes" or "no" is a thinking skill. It is also an incentive for returning books on time. It helps the librarian know how many students will be borrowing books, to know how much time to allow for book selection. It provides a check on students' borrowing habits. You may wish to design your own attendance words or invite the students to design some.

SEPTEMBER

Lesson 1

SKILL: Location of materials in the facility.

OBJECTIVE: Students will review where materials are located.

LITERATURE: "I Can Read" books in a series.

PREPARATION: A transparency of the activity "Parts of the Library." Overhead projector. Display "I Can Read" books in a series. Select one to use with class. Attendance roster. Story candle.

LESSON: Meet in story corner. Check attendance. Using transparency, have students find location of materials. Introduce "I Can Read" books. Introduce story, read and discuss. Tell briefly of books on display.

BOOK SELECTION: Students select one or two books. Return to story corner when books are signed out. Review lesson. Dismiss.

Lesson 2

SKILL: Care of library materials. Review of the parts of the books.

OBJECTIVE: Students will review care of library materials. Students will review spine, cover, pages, and dust jacket.

LITERATURE: "I Can Read" books by one author.

PREPARATION: A transparency of the activity "Mixed-up Words." Overhead projector. Display "I Can Read" books. Select one to use with the class.

LESSON: Meet in story corner.
Check attendance. Aster—books returned
Petunia—books not returned

Using transparency, complete activity as class. Introduce "I Can Read" series. Introduce story, read and discuss. Tell briefly of books on display.

BOOK SELECTION: Students return to story corner. Review lesson. Dismiss.

Lesson 3

SKILL: Knowledge and understanding of hardware and software.

OBJECTIVE: Students will review their knowledge of hardware and software.

LITERATURE: Nonfiction "I Can Read" books.

PREPARATION: A transparency of the activity "Hardware—Software." Overhead projector. Display nonfiction "I Can Read" books. Select one to use with the class.

LESSON: Meet in story corner.
       Check attendance. Aster—books returned
               Petunia—books not returned

Review hardware and software. Using transparency, complete activity as a class project. Introduce nonfiction "I Can Read" books. Introduce book, read and discuss. Tell briefly of books on display.

BOOK SELECTION: Students return to story corner. Review lesson. Dismiss.

Lesson 4

SKILL: Knowledge of concepts of author, title, illustrator, and illustrations.

OBJECTIVE: Students will review their knowledge of the concepts.

LITERATURE: "I Can Read" fiction and nonfiction.

PREPARATION: Display fiction and nonfiction "I Can Read" books. Select one to use with the class.

LESSON: Meet in story corner.
       Check attendance. Aster—books returned
               Petunia—books not returned

Review author, title, illustrator, and illustrations. Introduce story, read and discuss. Tell briefly of books on display.

BOOK SELECTION: Students return to story corner. Help students locate author, title, illustrator, and illustrations in their books. Review lesson. Dismiss.

PARTS OF THE LIBRARY

STORY CORNER

CIRCULATION DESK

RETURNING BOOKS TRUCK

PICTURE BOOKS

MAGAZINES

RECORDS

WORKROOM

DATE BOOKS ARE DUE

CARD CATALOG

REFERENCE SECTION

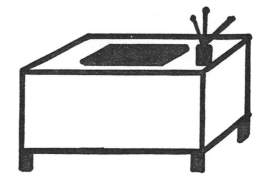

MIXED-UP WORDS

1. NIPSE   — — — — —

2. ROVEC   — — — — —

3. GAPES   — — — — —

4. TUSD KAJCTE   — — — —

— — — — — —

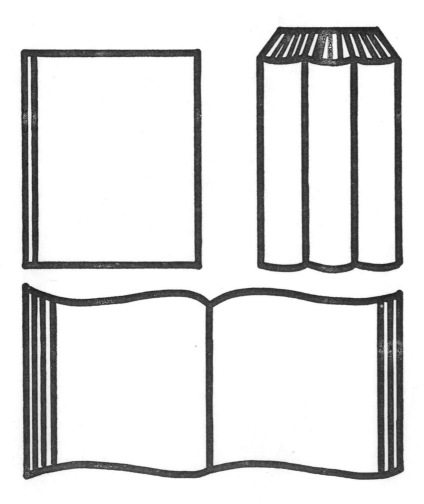

Name _____   Date _____

HARDWARE—SOFTWARE

DIRECTIONS: Label the hardware and software on the line beneath the picture.
Draw a line from each piece of hardware to its proper software.

1. _____

2. _____

3. _____

4. _____

5. _____

6. _____

7. _____

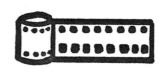

8. _____

9. _____

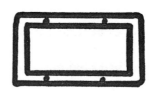

10. _____

OCTOBER

Lesson 1

SKILL: Knowledge and understanding of the book card, book pocket, and date due slip.

OBJECTIVE: Students will be introduced to the purpose of the book card, book pocket, and date due slip. Students will begin the process of signing out their own books.

LITERATURE: Mystery and detective fiction and nonfiction.

PREPARATION: Make a large model of the sheet "Book Card, Book Pocket, and Date Due Slip." Make copies of the practice book cards. Display a selection of mystery and detective fiction and nonfiction. Select one to use with the class.

LESSON: Meet in story corner.
Check attendance. Roses—books returned
Violets—books not returned

Using the model, introduce and explain book card, book pocket, and date due slip. Explain sign-out procedure. Show practice book cards. Practice book cards will be given to teachers to have students practice during the week and return next week. Introduce story, read, and discuss. Tell briefly of books on display.

BOOK SELECTION: Students return to story corner. Review lesson. Dismiss.

Lesson 2

SKILL: Knowledge and understanding of sign-out procedure.

OBJECTIVE: Students will begin to sign out their own books.

LITERATURE: Mystery and detective fiction and nonfiction.

PREPARATION: Large model of book card, book pocket, and date due slip. Display a selection of mystery and detective fiction and nonfiction. Select one to use with the class.

LESSON: Meet in story corner.
Check attendance. Roses—books returned
Violets—books not returned

Comment on practice book cards. Introduce story, read, discuss. Tell briefly of book on display. Students will sign out own books using practice book cards as example.

> *BOOK SELECTION:* Students return to story corner. Review lesson. Dismiss.

Lesson 3

SKILL: Knowledge and understanding of sign-out procedure.

OBJECTIVE: Students will sign out their own books.

LITERATURE: Mystery and detective fiction and nonfiction.

PREPARATION: Large model of book card, book pocket, and date due slip. Display a selection of mystery and detective fiction and nonfiction. Select one to use with the class.

LESSON: Meet in story corner.
　　　　Check attendance. Roses—books returned
　　　　　　　　Violets—books not returned

Comment on last week's sign-out. Commend if possible. Introduce story, read, discuss. Tell briefly of books on display.

BOOK SELECTION: Have students return to story corner. Review lesson. Dismiss.

Lesson 4

SKILL: Knowledge and understanding of sign-out procedure.

OBJECTIVE: All students will sign out own books properly.

LITERATURE: Mystery and detective fiction and nonfiction.

PREPARATION: Large model. Display a selection of mystery and detective fiction and nonfiction. Select one to use with the class.

LESSON: Meet in story corner.
　　　　Check attendance. Roses—books returned
　　　　　　　　Violets—books not returned

Discuss progress with sign-out procedure. Introduce story, read and discuss. Review sign-out procedure. Tell briefly of books on display.

BOOK SELECTION: Have students return to story corner. Discuss any problems with sign-out procedures. Students should be able to sign out own books from now on. Review lesson. Dismiss.

BOOK CARD, BOOK POCKET, AND DATE DUE SLIP

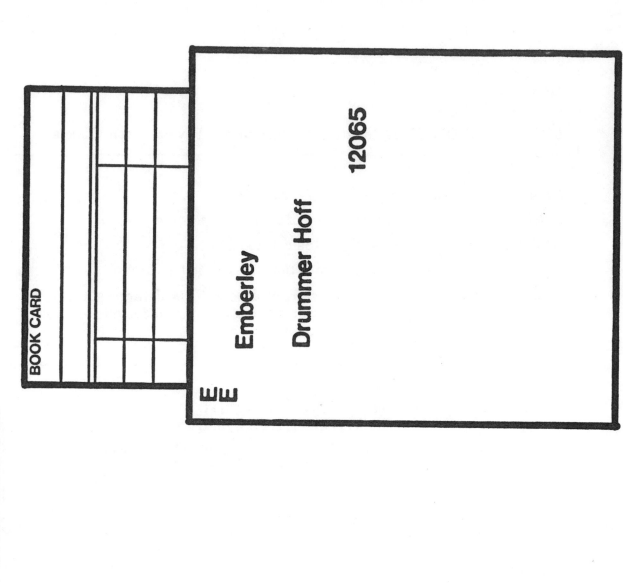

BOOK CARD

E
E Emberley

Drummer Hoff

12065

DATE DUE SLIP

BOOK CARDS

Author		
Title		
Date	**Name**	**Class**

Author		
Title		
Date	**Name**	**Class**

Author		
Title		
Date	**Name**	**Class**

Author		
Title		
Date	**Name**	**Class**

NOVEMBER

Lesson 1

SKILL: Knowledge and understanding of the concept of author, title, illustrator, illustrations, and publisher.

OBJECTIVE: Students will review the concepts. Students will be introduced to the concept of publisher.

LITERATURE: Animals. Farm animals—fiction and nonfiction.

PREPARATION: A copy of the concepts. Display a selection of books about farm animals, fiction and nonfiction. Select one to use with the class.

LESSON: Meet in story corner.
        Check attendance. Daisy—books returned
                Clover—books not returned

Review the concepts. Introduce and discuss publisher. Introduce story, read, and discuss. Tell briefly of books on display.

BOOK SELECTION: Students return to story corner. Help each student locate the publisher in own books. Review lesson. Dismiss.

Lesson 2

SKILL: Knowledge and understanding of the concept of author, title, illustrator, publisher, copyright, and copyright date.

OBJECTIVE: Students will review the concepts. Students will be introduced to copyright and copyright date.

LITERATURE: Animals. Zoo animals—fiction and nonfiction.

PREPARATION: A copy of the concepts. A large drawing of the copyright symbol. Display a selection of books about zoo animals, fiction and nonfiction. Select one to use with the class.

LESSON: Meet in story corner.
        Check attendance. Daisy—books returned
                Clover—books not returned

Review the concepts. Introduce and discuss copyright and copyright date. Introduce story, read, and discuss. Tell briefly of books on display.

BOOK SELECTION: Students return to story corner. Help students locate copyright date in their own books. Review lesson. Dismiss.

Lesson 3

SKILL: Knowledge and understanding of the concept of author, title, illustrator, illustrations, publisher, copyright, and copyright date.

OBJECTIVE: Students will review and reinforce their knowledge and understanding of the above concepts. Students will locate the copyright date in their own books.

LITERATURE: Animals. Water animals—fiction and nonfiction.

PREPARATION: A list of terms for the skill. A copy of the copyright symbol. Display a selection of books about water animals, fiction and nonfiction. Select one to use with the students.

LESSON: Meet in story corner.
Check attendance. Daisy—books returned
Clover—books not returned

Review the concepts. Review copyright and copyright date. Introduce story, read and discuss. Tell briefly of books on display.

BOOK SELECTION: Have students return to story corner. Have each student locate copyright date in own books. Review lesson. Dismiss.

Lesson 4

SKILL: Knowledge and understanding of the concepts.

OBJECTIVE: Each student will know and understand the concepts.

LITERATURE: Animals. Wild animals—fiction and nonfiction.

PREPARATION: A copy of the words and symbol. Display a selection of books about wild animals, fiction and nonfiction. Select one to use with the class.

LESSON: Students meet in story corner.
Check attendance. Daisy—books returned
Clover—books not returned

Using the copy of the words, review the concepts. Introduce story, read and discuss. Tell briefly of books on display.

BOOK SELECTION: Have students return to story corner. Have students locate the author, title, illustrator, publisher, and copyright date in their books. Help where needed. Review lesson. Dismiss.

DECEMBER

Lesson 1

SKILL: Correct spelling of the parts of the book.

OBJECTIVE: Students will practice the correct spelling of the terms; spine, cover, pages, and dust jacket.

LITERATURE: Fairy and folk tales. Seasonal fiction and nonfiction.

PREPARATION: A copy of each term. Display a selection of folk and fairy tales and/or seasonal fiction and nonfiction. Select one to use with the class.

LESSON: Meet in story corner.
Check attendance. Poinsettia—books returned
Ivy—books not returned

Give the definition of a term. Have student give term and spelling. Practice all terms several times. Introduce story, read and discuss. Tell briefly of books on display.

BOOK SELECTION: Students return to story corner. Review lesson. Dismiss.

Lesson 2

SKILL: Recognition and selection of the terms.

OBJECTIVE: Students will choose the correct term when given the definition.

LITERATURE: Fairy and folk tales. Seasonal fiction and nonfiction.

PREPARATION: Make a copy of the activity sheet "Choose the Term" for each group of 3 to 4 students. Laminate if possible. Cut and band together into packets. Display selection of folk and fairy tales and/or seasonal literature. Select one to use with the class.

LESSON: Meet in story corner.
Check attendance. Poinsettia—books returned
Ivy—books not returned

Divide class into groups. Give a packet to each group. Give definition. Group will select term and hold it up. Practice all terms several times. Collect packets. Introduce story, read and discuss. Tell briefly of books on display.

BOOK SELECTION: Students return to story corner. Review lesson. Dismiss.

Lesson 3

SKILL: Correct spelling of the concepts of the book.

OBJECTIVE: Students will practice the correct spelling of the concepts; author, title, illustrator, illustrations, publisher, and copyright date.

LITERATURE: Fairy and folk tales. Seasonal fiction and nonfiction.

PREPARATION: A copy of each term. Display a selection of fairy and folk tales and/or seasonal fiction and nonfiction.

LESSON: Meet in story corner.
Check attendance. Poinsettia—books returned
Ivy—books not returned

Give definition of term. Have students give definition and correct spelling. Practice all terms several times. Introduce story, read and discuss. Tell briefly of books on display.

BOOK SELECTION: Students return to story corner. Review lesson. Dismiss.

Lesson 4

SKILL: Recognition and selection of the concepts.

OBJECTIVE: Students will choose the correct concept when given the definition.

LITERATURE: Fairy and folk tales. Seasonal fiction and nonfiction.

PREPARATION: Make a copy of the activity sheet "Choose the Concept" for each group of 3 to 4 students. Laminate if possible. Cut and band together into packets. Display selection of fairy and folk tales and/or seasonal literature. Select one to use with the class.

LESSON: Meet in story corner.
Check attendance. Poinsettia—books returned
Ivy—books not returned

Divide class into groups. Give a packet to each group. Give definition. Group will select concept and hold it up. Practice all concepts several times. Collect packets. Introduce story, read and discuss. Tell briefly of books on display.

BOOK SELECTION: Students return to story corner. Review lesson. Dismiss.

SPINE

COVER

PAGES

DUST JACKET

CHOOSE THE CONCEPT

AUTHOR
TITLE
ILLUSTRATOR
ILLUSTRATIONS
PUBLISHER
COPYRIGHT DATE

JANUARY

Lesson 1

SKILL: Knowledge and understanding of alphabetizing and the call number.

OBJECTIVE: Students will practice alphabetizing. Students will be introduced to the concept of the call number.

LITERATURE: Contemporary fiction and nonfiction.

PREPARATION: A copy of the call number. Display a selection of contemporary fiction and nonfiction. Select one to use with the class.

LESSON: Meet in story corner.
Check attendance. Sunflower—books returned
Iris—books not returned

Review the alphabet. Introduce the call number. Discuss how fiction and nonfiction books are shelved. Show the spines of several books pointing out the call number for fiction and nonfiction. Introduce story, pointing out call number, read and discuss. Tell briefly of books on display.

BOOK SELECTION: Students return to story corner. Have students locate call number on their books. Dismiss.

Lesson 2

SKILL: Knowledge and understanding of alphabetizing and the call number.

OBJECTIVE: Students will review alphabetizing and the call number.

LITERATURE: Contemporary fiction and nonfiction.

PREPARATION: Make a transparency of the activity "How Books Are Shelved." Overhead projector. On 3 × 5 cards, write a letter on each card with an E above. Display a selection of contemporary fiction and nonfiction. Select one to use with the class.

LESSON: Meet in story corner.
Check attendance. Sunflower—books returned
Iris—books not returned

Using transparency, explain how E books are shelved. Ask where familiar authors' books would be shelved. Hand out cards. Each student will locate where that call number would be on the transparency. Introduce story, read and discuss. Tell briefly of books on display.

BOOK SELECTION: Students return to story corner. Review lesson. Dismiss.

Lesson 3

SKILL: Knowledge and understanding of alphabetizing and the call number.

OBJECTIVE: Students will review alphabetizing and the call number. Students will locate a specific call number on the shelves.

LITERATURE: Contemporary fiction and nonfiction.

PREPARATION: The 3 × 5 cards from last week's lesson. Access for all students to the E shelves. Display a selection of contemporary fiction and nonfiction. Select one to use with the class.

LESSON: Meet in story corner.
Check attendance. Sunflower—books returned
Iris—books not returned

Have class sit facing E shelves. Explain shelving. Hand out 3 × 5 cards. Have students locate the call number of their cards. In turn, each student will show where that call number is located. If there is time, introduce story, read and discuss. Tell briefly of books on display.

BOOK SELECTION: Students return to story corner. Have students locate call number on spine of their books. Dismiss.

Lesson 4

SKILL: Knowledge and understanding of alphabetizing and the call number.

OBJECTIVE: Students will review alphabetizing and the call number. Given the call number, students will begin locating their own books.

LITERATURE: Contemporary fiction and nonfiction.

PREPARATION: Twenty-six E books. Display a selection of contemporary fiction and nonfiction. Select one to use with the class.

LESSON: Meet in story corner.
Check attendance. Sunflower—books returned
Iris—books not returned

Have class move to E shelves. Review E shelving. Give each student a book. In turn, each student will tell the call number and shelve the book. Shelve extras as a class activity. If there is time, introduce story, read and discuss. Tell briefly of books on display.

BOOK SELECTION: Have students return to story corner. Review lesson. Dismiss.

HOW BOOKS ARE SHELVED

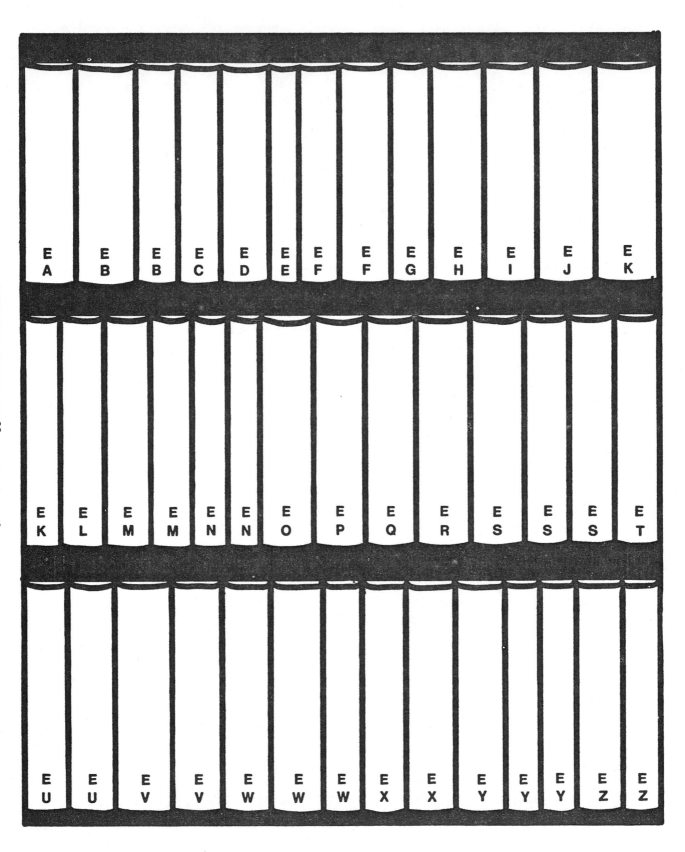

FEBRUARY

Lesson 1

SKILL: Knowledge and understanding of fiction and nonfiction.

OBJECTIVE: Students will be introduced to the difference between fiction and nonfiction.

LITERATURE: Historical fiction and nonfiction.

PREPARATION: A copy of the terms fiction and nonfiction. A selection of fiction and nonfiction for demonstration. Display a selection of historical fiction and nonfiction. Select one to use with the class.

LESSON: Meet in story corner.
Check attendance. Snapdragon—books returned
Marigold—books not returned

Introduce fiction and nonfiction. Think of fiction as "fake" and nonfiction as "not fake." Explain call number for fiction and nonfiction. Hold up each book and tell a bit about it. Have students decide whether it is fiction or nonfiction and why. Introduce story, read and discuss. Tell briefly of books on display.

BOOK SELECTION: Students return to story corner. Review lesson. Dismiss.

Lesson 2

SKILL: Knowledge and understanding of fiction and nonfiction.

OBJECTIVE: Students will reinforce their knowledge of fiction and nonfiction.

LITERATURE: Historical fiction and nonfiction.

PREPARATION: A copy of the terms fiction and nonfiction. Select two short pieces from a magazine, one fiction, one nonfiction. Display a selection of historical fiction and nonfiction. Select one to use with the class.

LESSON: Meet in story corner.
Check attendance. Snapdragon—books returned
Marigold—books not returned

Review fiction and nonfiction. Read the two pieces from magazine. Have students decide which is fiction, which is nonfiction. Introduce story, read and discuss. Tell briefly of books on display.

BOOK SELECTION: Students return to story corner. Review lesson. Dismiss.

Lesson 3

SKILL: Knowledge and understanding of fiction and nonfiction.

OBJECTIVE: Students will determine from the call number whether a book is fiction or nonfiction.

LITERATURE: Historical fiction and nonfiction.

PREPARATION: A copy of activity sheet "Fiction—Nonfiction" for each student. A box of crayons for each student. A transparency of activity. Overhead projector. Display a selection of fiction and nonfiction. Select one to use with the class.

LESSON: Meet in story corner.
Check attendance. Snapdragon—books returned
Marigold—books not returned

Have students move to tables. Hand out activity sheets and crayons. Using transparency, introduce activity. The activity may be completed independently or as a class project. If there is time, introduce, read and discuss story. Tell briefly of books on display.

BOOK SELECTION: Students return to story corner. Review lesson. Dismiss.

Lesson 4

SKILL: Knowledge and understanding of fiction and nonfiction.

OBJECTIVE: Students will reinforce their knowledge of fiction and nonfiction.

LITERATURE: Historical fiction and nonfiction.

PREPARATION: A transparency of the activity "Shelving Fiction and Nonfiction." A transparency of the activity "Fiction—nonfiction." Cut the spines of the books apart. Overhead projector. Display a selection of historical fiction and nonfiction. Select one to use with the class.

LESSON: Meet in story corner.
Check attendance. Snapdragon—books returned
Marigold—books not returned

Review fiction and nonfiction. Using transparency, complete activity with class. Introduce story, read and discuss. Tell briefly of books on display.

BOOK SELECTION: Students return to story corner. Review lesson. Dismiss.

Name _____

Date _____

FICTION—NONFICTION

Color the spines of the FICTION books BLUE. Color the spines of the NONFICTION books RED.

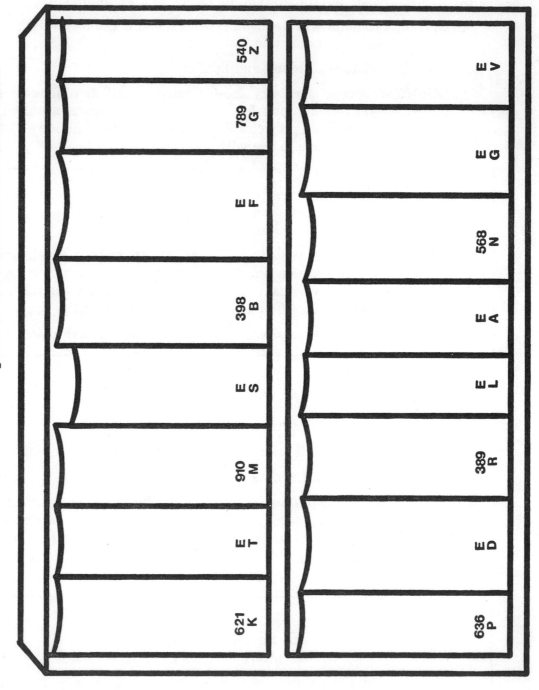

Name _____   Date _____

SHELVING FICTION AND NONFICTION BOOKS

Cut out the spines from the "Fiction—Nonfiction" activity sheet. Place the spines on the proper shelf in the proper order.

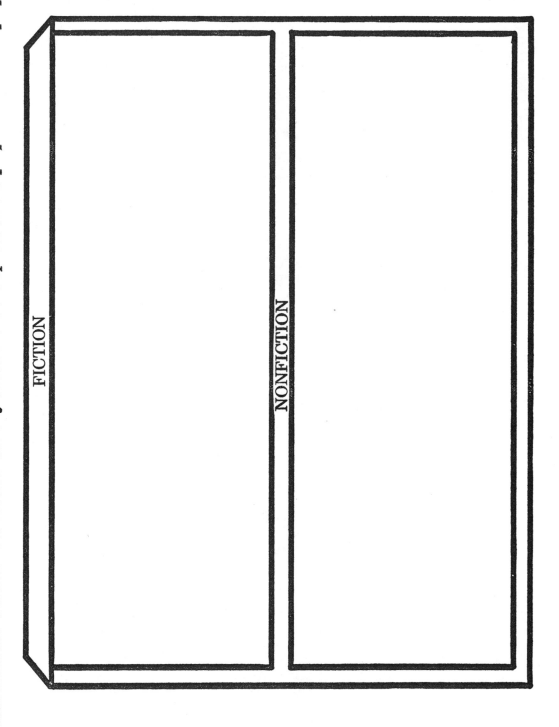

FICTION

NONFICTION

MARCH

Lesson 1

SKILL: Knowledge and understanding of the elements of a story: the characters.

OBJECTIVE: Students will be introduced to the concept of characters.

LITERATURE: Realistic problem solving fiction and nonfiction.

PREPARATION: A copy of the phrase, Elements of a Story. A copy of the term "characters." Display a selection of realistic fiction and nonfiction. Select one to use with the class.

LESSON: Meet in story corner.
Check attendance. Daffodil—books returned
Lily—books not returned

Using the terms, introduce and discuss characters. Introduce story, read and discuss. Tell briefly of books on display.

BOOK SELECTION: Students return to story corner. Review lesson. Dismiss.

Lesson 2

SKILL: Knowledge and understanding of the elements of a story: main character and supporting characters.

OBJECTIVE: Students will review the meaning of characters. Students will be introduced to the terms "main characters" and "supporting characters."

LITERATURE: Realistic fiction and nonfiction.

PREPARATION: A copy of the phrase, Elements of a Story. A copy of the term "characters." A copy of the terms "main character" and "supporting characters." Display a selection of realistic fiction and nonfiction. Select one to use with the class.

LESSON: Meet in story corner.
Check attendance. Daffodil—books returned
Lily—books not returned

Using copy of terms, review characters as elements of a story. Introduce, explain, and discuss main character and supporting characters. Introduce story, read and discuss story, emphasizing characters. Tell briefly of books on display.

BOOK SELECTION: Students return to story corner. Review lesson. Dismiss.

Lesson 3

SKILL: Knowledge and understanding of the elements of a story: the characters, the main character, and the supporting characters.

OBJECTIVE: Students will reinforce their understanding of the main character and the supporting characters.

LITERATURE: Realistic fiction and nonfiction.

PREPARATION: A copy of the term Elements of a Story, characters, main character, and supporting characters. Select several books familiar to the entire class. Display a selection of realistic fiction and nonfiction. Select one to use with the class.

LESSON: Meet in story corner.
Check attendance. Daffodil—books returned
Lily—books not returned

Review the concepts. Using pre-selected books, have students determine: characters, main character, and supporting characters. Introduce story, read and discuss. Tell briefly of books on display.

BOOK SELECTION: Students return to story corner. Review lesson. Dismiss.

Lesson 4

SKILL: Knowledge and understanding of the elements of a story: characters, main character, and supporting characters.

OBJECTIVE: Students will recall the characters, the main character, and the supporting characters in one book read during the week.

LITERATURE: Realistic fiction and nonfiction.

PREPARATION: A transparency of the activity "Who's Who." Overhead projector. Display a selection of realistic fiction and nonfiction. Select one to use with the class.

LESSON: Meet students at the door. Have them bring one book to the story corner.
Check attendance. Daffodil—books returned
Lily—books not returned

Review concepts. Using transparency, have each student give the information for the activity from the book. Help where needed. If time, introduce, read and discuss story. Tell briefly of books on display.

BOOK SELECTION: Students return to story corner. Review lesson. Dismiss.

Name ——

Date ——

WHO'S WHO

STUDENT	AUTHOR AND TITLE	MAIN CHARACTER	SUPPORTING CHARACTERS	CALL NUMBER

APRIL

Lesson 1

SKILL: Knowledge and understanding of the elements of a story: the setting.

OBJECTIVE: Students will be introduced to the concept of setting.

LITERATURE: Foreign setting fiction and nonfiction.

PREPARATION: A copy of the phrase Elements of a Story. A copy of the term "characters." A copy of the term "setting." Display a selection of foreign setting fiction and nonfiction. Select one to use with the class.

LESSON: Meet in story corner.
    Check attendance. Tulip—books returned
                  Hollyhock—books not returned

Using Elements of a Story, briefly review characters. Introduce and discuss setting. Introduce story, read and discuss. Tell briefly of books on display.

BOOK SELECTION: Students return to story corner. Review lesson. Dismiss.

Lesson 2

SKILL: Knowledge and understanding of the elements of a story: the setting.

OBJECTIVE: Students will become familiar with the concept of setting and will begin determining the setting of a story.

LITERATURE: Foreign setting fiction and nonfiction.

PREPARATION: A copy of the phrase "Elements of a Story." A copy of the term "characters." A copy of the term "setting." Display a selection of foreign setting fiction and nonfiction. Select one to use with the class.

LESSON: Meet class at the door. Have students bring all returning fiction to the story corner.
    Check attendance. Tulip—books returned
                  Hollyhock—books not returned

Review the concepts. Have students with fiction books show the book, tell the characters, main and supporting, and the setting. Help where needed. Collect books to be carded and placed on display. Introduce, read and discuss story. Tell briefly of books on display.

> *BOOK SELECTION:* Students return to story corner. Review lesson. Dismiss.

Lesson 3

SKILL: Knowledge and understanding of the elements of a story: the plot.

OBJECTIVE: Students will be introduced to the concept of plot.

LITERATURE: Foreign setting fiction and nonfiction.

PREPARATION: A copy of the phrase "Elements of a Story." A copy of the term "plot." Display a selection of foreign setting fiction and nonfiction. Select one to use with the class.

LESSON: Meet in story corner.
Check attendance. Tulip—books returned
Hollyhock—books not returned

Using Elements of a Story, review concept of characters and setting. Introduce and discuss plot. Introduce, read and discuss story. Bring in plot. Tell briefly of books on display.

BOOK SELECTION: Students return to story corner. Review lesson. Dismiss.

Lesson 4

SKILL: Knowledge and understanding of the elements of a story: the plot.

OBJECTIVE: Students will become familiar with the concept of plot and will begin determining the plot of a story.

LITERATURE: Foreign setting fiction and nonfiction.

PREPARATION: A copy of the phrase "Elements of a Story." A copy of the term "plot." Display a selection of foreign setting fiction and nonfiction. Select one to use with the class.

LESSON: Meet the class at the door. Have students bring all returning fiction to story corner.
Check attendance. Tulip—books returned
Hollyhock—books not returned

Review plot. Ask students with fiction to tell the plot of their books. Collect books to be carded and displayed. Introduce, read and discuss story. Tell briefly of books on display.

BOOK SELECTION: Students return to story corner. Review lesson. Dismiss.

MAY

Lesson 1

SKILL: Knowledge and understanding of the three parts of a story: the beginning, the middle, and the end.

OBJECTIVE: Students will be introduced to the concept that a story has three parts: the beginning, the middle, and the end.

LITERATURE: Humorous fiction and nonfiction.

PREPARATION: A copy of the phrase "The Three Parts of a Story." A copy of the terms "beginning," "middle," and "end." Select several books familiar to all students. Display a selection of humorous fiction and nonfiction. Select one to use with the class.

LESSON: Meet in story corner.
Check attendance. Black-eyed Susan—books returned
Butter and eggs—books not returned

Using phrase and terms, introduce and discuss the three parts of a story. Using preselected books, explain and discuss the three parts of each. Introduce story, read and discuss, emphasizing the three parts of the story. Tell briefly of books on display.

BOOK SELECTION: Students return to story corner. Review lesson. Dismiss.

Lesson 2

SKILL: Knowledge and understanding of the three parts of a story: the beginning, the middle, and the end.

OBJECTIVE: Students will review and reinforce their knowledge of the concept that a story has three parts.

LITERATURE: Humorous fiction and nonfiction.

PREPARATION: A copy of the phrase "The Three Parts of a Story." A copy of the terms "beginning," "middle," and "end." Display a selection of humorous fiction and nonfiction. Select one to use with the class.

LESSON: Meet in story corner.
Check attendance. Black-eyed Susan—books returned
Butter and eggs—books not returned

Using the copy of the concepts, review the three parts of a story and what happens in each part. Introduce story, read and discuss, emphasizing the three parts. Tell briefly of books on display.

BOOK SELECTION: Students return to story corner. Review lesson. Dismiss.

Lesson 3

SKILL: Knowledge and understanding of the three parts of a story: the beginning, the middle, and the end.

OBJECTIVE: Students will practice the three parts of a story.

LITERATURE: Humorous fiction and nonfiction.

PREPARATION: A copy of the phrase "The Three Parts of a Story." A copy of the terms "beginning," "middle," and "end." Display a selection of humorous fiction and nonfiction. Select one to use with the class.

LESSON: Meet students at the door. Have students each bring one fiction book being returned to story corner.
Check attendance. Black-eyed Susan—books returned
Butter and eggs—books not returned

Using the phrase, review the three parts of a story. Have students volunteer to tell the plot in the three parts of the story. Collect books to be carded and displayed. Introduce, read and discuss story. Tell briefly of books on display.

BOOK SELECTION: Students return to story corner. Review lesson. Dismiss.

Lesson 4

SKILL: Knowledge and understanding of the three parts of a story: the beginning, the middle, and the end.

OBJECTIVE: Students will practice the three parts of a story.

LITERATURE: Humorous fiction and nonfiction.

PREPARATION: A copy of the phrase "The Three Parts of a Story." A copy of the terms "beginning," "middle," and "end." Display a selection of humorous fiction and nonfiction. Select one to use with the class.

LESSON: Meet students at the door. Have students each bring one fiction book being returned to the story corner.
Check attendance. Black-eyed Susan—books returned
Butter and eggs—books not returned

Using the phrase and terms, review the three parts of a story. Have students who did not have a turn last week volunteer to tell the plot in the three parts of the story.

BOOK SELECTION: Students return to story corner. Review lesson. Dismiss.

JUNE

Lesson 1

SKILL: Knowledge and understanding of the following terms: reader, book, spine, cover, pages, author, title, publisher, copyright, and copyright date.

OBJECTIVE: Students will complete an activity designed to review their knowledge of the parts of the book.

LITERATURE: Poetry and stories in rhyme.

PREPARATION: A transparency of the activity sheet "Puzzling Words." Overhead projector. Display a selection of poetry and stories in rhyme. Select one to use with the class.

LESSON: Meet in story corner.
Check attendance. Dandelion—books returned
Gladiolus—books not returned

Using transparency, read the clues to the students. Have them figure out the answer. Introduce, read and discuss story. Tell briefly of books on display.

BOOK SELECTION: Students return to story corner. Review lesson. Dismiss.

Lesson 2

SKILL: Knowledge and understanding of the terms: book card, book pocket, and date due slip.

OBJECTIVE: Students will review and reinforce their knowledge of the book card, book pocket, and date due slip.

LITERATURE: Poetry and stories in rhyme.

PREPARATION: Large model of book card, book pocket, and date due slip. Display a selection of poetry and stories in rhyme. Select one to use with the class.

LESSON: Meet in story corner.
              Check attendance. Dandelion—books returned
                               Gladiolus—books not returned

              Using large model, review purpose of book card, book pocket, and date due slip. If your students use a public library, discuss the differences in checkout procedures. Introduce, read and discuss story. Tell briefly of books on display.

BOOK SELECTION: Students return to story corner. Review lesson. Dismiss.

Lesson 3

SKILL: Knowledge and understanding of the terms and concepts introduced during the year.

OBJECTIVE: Students will recall terms and concepts introduced during the year.

LITERATURE: Poetry and stories in rhyme.

PREPARATION: A copy of "Terms and Concepts Covered During the Year." A blank transparency. Display a selection of poetry and stories in rhyme. Select one to use with the class.

LESSON: Meet in story corner.
              Check attendance. Dandelion—books returned
                               Gladiolus—books not returned

              Using blank transparency, have students name all the terms and concepts covered during the year. Compare with the list. Introduce story, read and discuss. Tell briefly of books on display.

BOOK SELECTION: Students return to story corner. Review lesson. Dismiss.

Lesson 4

SKILL: Recall of authors and titles.

OBJECTIVE: Students will recall authors and titles of books read during the year.

LITERATURE: Poetry and stories in rhyme.

PREPARATION: Display board or easel. Several large sheets of paper and a pen. Select a book or filmstrip to use with the class.

LESSON: Meet in story corner.
Check attendance. Dandelion—books returned
Gladiolus—books not returned

Write "author" at the top of the paper. Have students think of as many authors as possible. Write "title" at the top of paper. Have students think of as many titles as possible. Introduce story, read and discuss. As this is the last lesson, there will be no book selection. Discuss any summer reading programs available to the students. Dismiss.

PUZZLING WORDS

1. What a person reads.   BOKO   _____

2. The backbone of the book.   NIEPS   _____

3. What the words are written on. SPEAG   _____

4. The person who reads a book.   DEARRE   _____

5. The person who writes a book.   RAUTHO   _____

6. The name of the book.   LITTE   _____

7. The outside boards of the book. ROVEC   _____

8. The person who draws the pictures. TRATILLUSOR   _____

9. The company that prints the book. SHIPUBLER   _____

10. Permission to publish a book. PROGTHICY   _____

11. The date the book is published. GRICOPHTY TADE   _____

Name _____   Date _____

TERMS AND CONCEPTS COVERED DURING
THE YEAR

SPINE   COVER   PAGES   DUST JACKET

AUTHOR   TITLE   ILLUSTRATOR   ILLUSTRATIONS

FILMSTRIP PROJECTOR   PHONOGRAPH OR

   RECORD PROJECTOR   CASSETTE PLAYER/RECORDER

FILMSTRIP   RECORD   CASSETTE   TRANSPARENCY   DISK

LIBRARY/MEDIA CENTER   CIRCULATION DESK

BOOK CARD   BOOK POCKET   DATE DUE SLIP

PUBLISHER

COPYRIGHT   COPYRIGHT DATE

CHARACTERS   MAIN CHARACTER   SUPPORTING CHARACTERS

CALL NUMBER

FICTION   NONFICTION

SETTING   PLOT

SECTIONS OF A STORY:

   BEGINNING

   MIDDLE

   END

GRADE 2

OVERVIEW

The main objectives in second grade are:

- to build a solid background of information regarding terms and concepts as a prerequisite to the formal teaching of information and retrieval skills.
- to review and reinforce the terms and concepts through use.
- to introduce the arrangement of fiction and nonfiction.
- to introduce special areas of literature.

Terms and Concepts To Be Reviewed and Reinforced

Regulations and procedures of the facility.

Author, Title, Illustrator, Illustrations, Publisher, Copyright, Copyright Date.

Spine, Cover, Pages, Dust Jacket.

Characters, Main Character, Supporting Characters, Setting, Plot

Parts of a story: Beginning, Middle, End

Fiction, Nonfiction

Terms and Concepts To Be Introduced

Place of Publication, Dedication Page, Title Page

Medium and mood of illustration

Biography, Autobiography, Collective Biography

Dewey Decimal System

Arrangement of fiction and nonfiction

Literature

Around-the-world folk tales

Mystery and Detective

Seasonal

Historical

Caldecott Award

Biography

American Tall Tales

Fiction (Authors such as Cleary, Haywood, Chew, etc.)
Magazines

Attendance

Taking attendance adds importance to the class. It helps the librarian learn the students' full names quicker. It also provides a record of who was absent when a certain concept or skill was introduced.

Special Words for Attendance

Using special words during attendance to determine whether students returned their books rather than "yes" or "no" is a thinking skill. It is also an incentive to return books on time. It helps the librarian to know how many students will be checking out books, to know how much time will be needed for book selection. If a student did not borrow books, the term is always "no books." It keeps a check on students borrowing habits. You may wish to create your own words or invite students to create words—one positive, one negative.

Special Activities

The following activities should be correlated with the classroom. All activities should be planned jointly by the librarian and classroom teacher.

Caldecott Unit
Tall Tale Unit
Magazine Unit

SEPTEMBER

Lesson 1

SKILL: Knowledge and understanding of library regulations and procedures. Knowledge and understanding of the various sections of the library.

OBJECTIVE: Students will review library procedures and location of materials.

LITERATURE: World folklore.

PREPARATION: Two copies each of activity "Where Do We Live?" Laminate each set. Place one set in proper places. Keep one set for class. Large model of book card, book pocket, and date due slip. A map of the world. Display a selection of folklore from a country. Select one to use with the class. Roster of students' names in attendance book.

> *LESSON:* Meet in story corner.
> Check attendance. Apple—books returned
> Banana—books not returned
>
> Discuss location of materials. Divide class into six groups. Give each group a card. Each group will locate the proper place by matching the card. Each group will tell the other groups where the materials are located. Using world map, introduce folk tale, read and discuss. Review borrowing procedures. Tell briefly of books on display.
>
> *BOOK SELECTION:* Students return to story corner. Review lesson. Dismiss.

Lesson 2

SKILL: Concept of author, title, illustrator, publisher, copyright date, and place of publication.

OBJECTIVE: Students will review and reinforce their knowledge of the concepts.

LITERATURE: World folklore.

PREPARATION: Map of the world. Display a selection of folklore from another country. Select one to use with the class.

> *LESSON:* Meet in story corner.
> Check attendance. Apple—books returned
> Banana—books not returned
>
> Discuss and review the concepts. Introduce and discuss place of publication. Introduce folk tale. Locate country on map. Read and discuss. Tell briefly of books on display.
>
> *BOOK SELECTION:* Students return to story corner. Review lesson. Dismiss.

Lesson 3

SKILL: Knowledge and understanding of the parts of the book: spine, cover, pages, illustrations, dust jacket, property stamp, and accession number.

OBJECTIVE: Students will review the parts of the book. Students will be introduced to the property stamp and the accession number.

LITERATURE: World folklore.

PREPARATION: A book with a dust jacket for each student. One for demonstration. Wall map. Display a selection of folklore from a country. Select one to use with the class.

LESSON: Meet in story corner.
Check attendance. Apple—books returned
Banana—books not returned

Give each student a book. Have students place hand on each part of the book as you name each part. Introduce and discuss property stamp and accession number. Introduce folk tale and country, read and discuss. Tell briefly of books on display.

BOOK SELECTION: Students return to story corner. Review lesson. Dismiss.

Lesson 4

SKILL: Knowledge and understanding of the elements of a story: characters, setting, and plot; and the three parts of a story: the beginning, the middle, and the end.

OBJECTIVE: Students will review and reinforce their knowledge of the concepts.

LITERATURE: World folklore.

PREPARATION: A world map. Display a selection of folklore from a country or continent. Select one to use with the class.

LESSON: Meet in story corner.
Check attendance. Apple—books returned
Banana—books not returned

Review and discuss the elements of a story. Review and discuss the three parts of a story. Introduce folk tale and country, read and discuss. Tell briefly of books on display.

BOOK SELECTION: Students return to story corner. Review lesson. Dismiss.

WHERE DO WE LIVE? #1

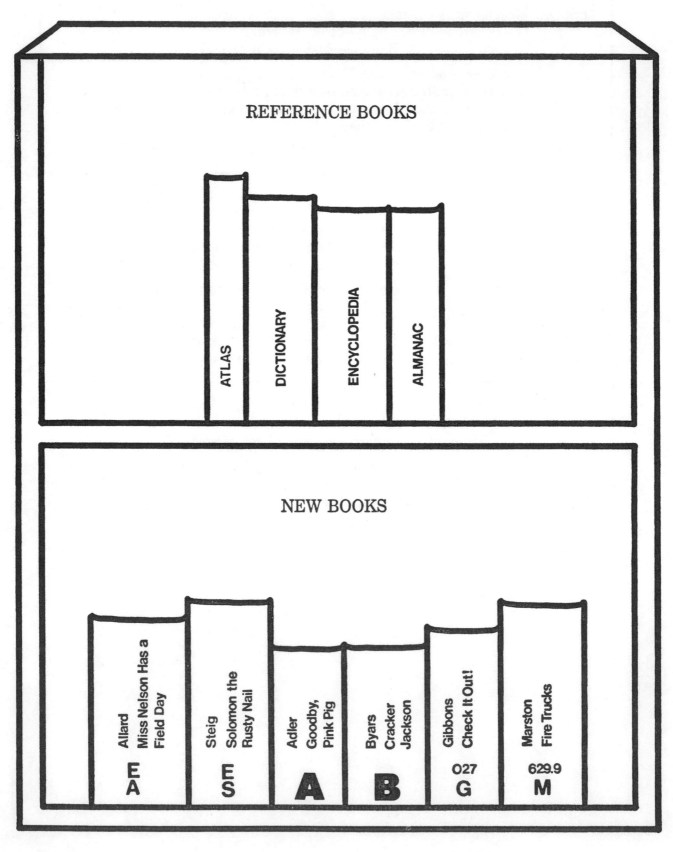

WHERE DO WE LIVE? #2

MAGAZINES

RECORDS AND TAPES

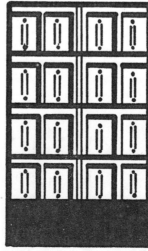

Name _____   Date _____

WHERE DO WE LIVE? #3

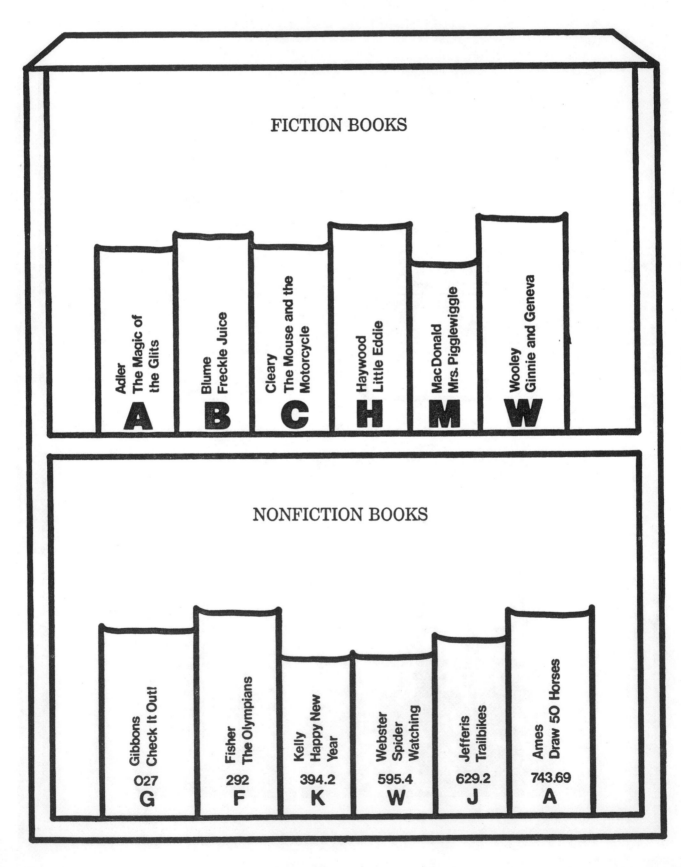

FICTION BOOKS

Adler
The Magic of
the Glits
A

Blume
Freckle Juice
B

Cleary
The Mouse and the
Motorcycle
C

Haywood
Little Eddie
H

MacDonald
Mrs. Pigglewiggle
M

Wooley
Ginnie and Geneva
W

NONFICTION BOOKS

Gibbons
Check It Out!
027
G

Fisher
The Olympians
292
F

Kelly
Happy New
Year
394.2
K

Webster
Spider
Watching
595.4
W

Jefferis
Trailbikes
629.2
J

Ames
Draw 50 Horses
743.69
A

WHERE DO WE LIVE? #4

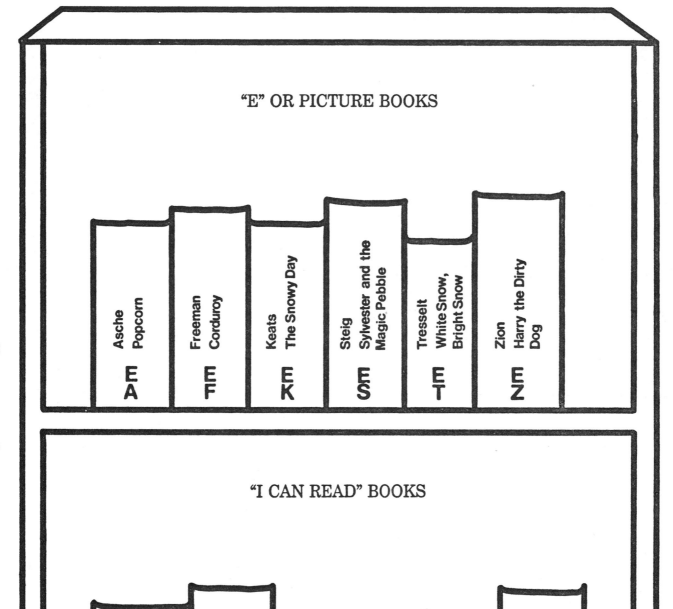

"E" OR PICTURE BOOKS

Asche
Popcorn
E A

Freeman
Corduroy
E F

Keats
The Snowy Day
E K

Steig
Sylvester and the
Magic Pebble
E S

Tresselt
White Snow,
Bright Snow
E T

Zion
Harry the Dirty
Dog
E N

"I CAN READ" BOOKS

Berenstain
The Bears'
Picnic
E B

Hoff
Danny and the
Dinosaur
E H

Hurd
Stop, Stop,
Stop
E H

Minerick
Cat and Dog
E M

Parish
No More Monsters
for Me
P P

Seuss
The Cat in the Hat
E S

OCTOBER

Lesson 1

SKILL: Knowledge and understanding of the title page.

OBJECTIVE: Students will be introduced to the title page.

LITERATURE: Mystery and detective fiction and nonfiction.

PREPARATION: Photocopy title page and verso page of 4 to 5 books, including fiction, nonfiction, and easy. Make transparencies from photocopies. Overhead projector. Display a selection of mystery and detective fiction and nonfiction. Select one to use with the class.

LESSON: Meet in story corner.
　　　　　Check attendance. Raspberry—books returned
　　　　　　　　　　　　　　Pineapple—books not returned

Using transparencies, introduce the title page, the information found on the title page, and the order of the information. Introduce story, emphasizing title page, read and discuss. Tell briefly of books on display.

BOOK SELECTION: Students return to story corner and locate title page in their own books. Review lesson. Dismiss.

Lesson 2

SKILL: Knowledge and understanding of the information on the title page.

OBJECTIVE: Students will practice decoding the information on a title page.

LITERATURE: Mystery and detective fiction and nonfiction.

PREPARATION: Transparencies from last week's lessons. Overhead projector. Display a selection of mystery and detective fiction and nonfiction. Select one to use with the class.

LESSON: Meet in story corner.
　　　　　Check attendance. Raspberry—books returned
　　　　　　　　　　　　　　Pineapple—books not returned

Using transparencies, practice decoding the information on a title page. Introduce this week's story, read and discuss. Tell briefly of books on display.

BOOK SELECTION: Students return to story corner. Have students find title page in their books. Review lesson. Dismiss.

Lesson 3

SKILL: Knowledge and understanding of the title page and parts of the book.

OBJECTIVE: Students will complete an activity designed to practice locating the title page and parts of the book.

LITERATURE: Mystery and detective fiction and nonfiction.

PREPARATION: A copy of "Parts of the Book" for each student. A box of crayons for each student. A copy of the directions. Display a selection of mystery and detective fiction and nonfiction. Select one to use with the class if time allows.

LESSON: Meet in story corner.
Check attendance. Raspberry—books returned
Pineapple—books not returned

Move to tables. Hand out materials. Following activity directions, have students complete activity. If there is time, return to story corner. Introduce, read and discuss a story. Tell briefly of books on display.

BOOK SELECTION: Students return to story corner. Review lesson. Dismiss.

Lesson 4

SKILL: Knowledge and understanding of the title page.

OBJECTIVE: Students will design an original title page.

LITERATURE: Mystery and detective fiction and nonfiction.

PREPARATION: A copy of the activity "Title Page" for each student. A box of crayons for each student. Transparencies of title page. Overhead projector. Display a selection of mystery and detective fiction and nonfiction. Select one to use with the class if time allows.

LESSON: Meet in story corner.
Check attendance. Raspberry—books returned
Pineapple—books not returned

Move to tables. Hand out materials. Using transparencies, introduce and explain activity. Have students complete activity. If there is time, return to story corner. Introduce story, read and discuss. Tell briefly of books on display.

BOOK SELECTION: Students return to story corner. Review title page. Dismiss.

DIRECTIONS FOR
PARTS OF THE BOOK

MATERIALS NEEDED: A copy of the activity sheet "Parts of the Book" and a box of crayons containing red, orange, yellow, green, blue, brown, and black for each student.

DIRECTIONS TO STUDENTS:

1. Pick up your red crayon. Find the spine of the book *WHERE THE WILD THINGS ARE.* Color the spine red. Put down your red crayon.

2. Pick up your brown crayon. Find the squirrel on the title page. Color the squirrel brown. Put down your brown crayon.

3. Pick up your yellow crayon. Find the spine of the book *THE SNOWY DAY.* Color the spine yellow. Put down your yellow crayon.

4. Pick up your black crayon. Find the title *WINTER'S SNACK* on the title page. Draw a black circle around the title. Put down your black crayon.

5. Pick up your orange crayon. Find the title *WINTER'S SNACK* on the cover. Draw an orange circle around the title. Put down your orange crayon.

6. Pick up your green crayon. Find the spine of the book *DRUMMER HOFF.* Color the spine green. Put down your green crayon.

7. Pick up your purple crayon. Find the squirrel on the front cover of the book *WINTER'S SNACK.* Color the squirrel purple. Put down your purple crayon.

8. Pick up your red crayon. Find the word *PUBLISHER* on the lower right outside the title page. Draw a red circle around the word. Now go to your left and find the publisher's name on the title page *UNITED HOUSE, INC. BRISTOL, RI.* Color a red circle around the publisher's name. Put down your red crayon.

9. Pick up your blue crayon. Find the word *AUTHOR* on the lower right outside edge of the title page. Draw a blue circle around the word. Now go to your left and find the author *ANNE JONES* on the title page. Draw a blue circle around the author's name. Put down your blue crayon.

10. Pick up your purple crayon. Find the word *ILLUSTRATOR* on the lower right outside the title page. Now go to the left and find the illustrator *JOHN BROWN* on the title page. Draw a purple circle around the illustrator's name. Put down your purple crayon.

11. Pick up your green crayon. Find the words *TITLE PAGE* beneath the picture of the title page. Draw a green circle around the words. Put down your green crayon.

DIRECTIONS FOR PARTS OF THE BOOK (continued)

12. Pick up your black crayon. Find the author *SENDAK* on the spine of the book *WHERE THE WILD THINGS ARE.* Draw a black circle around the author's name. Put down your black crayon.

13. Pick up your orange crayon. Find the author *EMBERLEY* on the spine of the book *DRUMMER HOFF.* Draw an orange circle around the author's name. Put down your orange crayon.

14. Pick up your brown crayon. Find the author *KEATS* on the spine of the book *THE SNOWY DAY.* Draw a brown circle around the author's name. Put down your brown crayon.

15. Pick up your favorite color. Write your name and today's date on the lines at the bottom of the page next to where it says *NAME AND DATE.*

Name _____   Date _____

PARTS OF THE BOOK

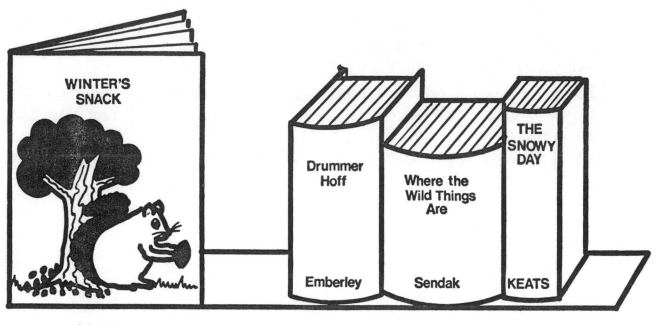

COVER   SPINE

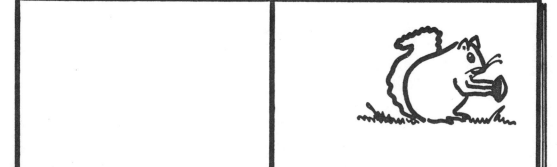

WINTER'S SNACK   Title

BY: ANNE JONES   Author

PICTURES BY: JOHN BROWN   Illustrator

UNITED HOUSE, INC., BRISTOL, RI   Publisher

TITLE PAGE

Name _____ Date _____

THE TITLE PAGE

DIRECTIONS: Design a *TITLE PAGE*. Be sure to include: author, title, illustrator, place of publication, and copyright date.

Author _____

Title _____

Illustrator _____

Publisher _____

Place of publication _____ Copyright date _____

NOVEMBER

Lesson 1

SKILL: Knowledge and understanding of the dedication page.

OBJECTIVE: Students will be introduced to the dedication page.

LITERATURE: Historical fiction and nonfiction.

PREPARATION: A copy of the term "dedication page." Select 4 to 5 books with dedication pages. Display a selection of historical fiction and nonfiction. Select one to use with the class.

LESSON: Meet in story corner.
Check attendance. Oranges—books returned
Nuts—books not returned

Using term, introduce dedication page. Explain purpose. Read the dedication from selected books and discuss. Introduce story, read and discuss. Tell briefly of books on display.

BOOK SELECTION: Students return to story corner. Have students look for a dedication in their books. Review lesson. Dismiss.

Lesson 2

SKILL: Knowledge and understanding of the dedication page.

OBJECTIVE: Students will be able to locate the dedication in a book.

LITERATURE: Historical fiction and nonfiction.

PREPARATION: A copy of the term dedication page. Display a selection of historical fiction and nonfiction. Select one to use with the class.

LESSON: Meet in story corner.
Check attendance. Oranges—books returned
Nuts—books not returned

Review dedication page. Introduce story, read and discuss. Tell briefly of books on display.

BOOK SELECTION: Students return to story corner. Have students check for dedication in their books. Have students read the dedications to the class. Review lesson. Dismiss.

Lesson 3

SKILL: Knowledge and understanding of fiction and nonfiction.

OBJECTIVE: Students will review and reinforce their ability to differentiate between fiction and nonfiction.

LITERATURE: Historical fiction and nonfiction.

PREPARATION: A copy of the terms fiction and nonfiction. Display a selection of historical fiction and nonfiction. Select one to use with the class.

LESSON: Meet in story corner.
Check attendance. Oranges—books returned
Nuts—books not returned

Using terms, review fiction and nonfiction. Students will be expected to use terms when asking for books. Introduce story, read and discuss. Tell briefly of books on display.

BOOK SELECTION: Students return to story corner. Have students check to determine whether their books are fiction or nonfiction. Review lesson. Dismiss.

Lesson 4

SKILL: Knowledge and understanding of fiction and nonfiction.

OBJECTIVE: Students will determine whether a book is fiction or nonfiction through listening to a synopsis of the book.

LITERATURE: Historical fiction and nonfiction.

PREPARATION: Select 4 to 5 books, without pictures on covers, of which a brief synopsis can be given. Display a selection of historical fiction and nonfiction. Select one to use with the class.

LESSON: Meet in story corner.
Check attendance. Oranges—books returned
Nuts—books not returned

Using terms, review fiction and nonfiction. Give a synopsis of each book and have students determine whether each is fiction or nonfiction. Introduce story, read and discuss. Tell briefly of books on display.

BOOK SELECTION: Students return to story corner. Have students determine whether their books are fiction or nonfiction. Review lesson. Dismiss.

DECEMBER

Lesson 1

SKILL: Identifying different types of mediums.

OBJECTIVE: Students will be introduced to collages and photographs as mediums of illustrations.

LITERATURE: Books using collages and photographs as illustrations. Seasonal fiction and nonfiction.

PREPARATION: Make a copy of the terms "collage" and "photographs," and of the information sheet. Select several books using collages and several books using photographs for demonstration. Display a selection of books using collages and photographs as well as seasonal fiction and nonfiction. Select one to use with the class.

LESSON: Meet in story corner.
  Check attendance. Cranberry—books returned
    Limes—books not returned

Introduce and discuss collages and photographs as mediums of illustration. Show selected books. Introduce story, read and discuss. Tell briefly of books on display.

BOOK SELECTION: Students return to story corner. Review lesson. Dismiss.

Lesson 2

SKILL: Identifying different mediums of illustrations.

OBJECTIVE: Students will review collages and photographs. Students will be introduced to watercolors and woodcuts as illustrations.

LITERATURE: Books using watercolors and woodcuts as illustrations. Seasonal fiction and nonfiction.

PREPARATION: Make a copy of the terms "watercolors," "woodcuts," "collages," and "photographs." Have a copy of the information sheet. Display a selection of books using watercolors and woodcuts as illustrations. Display seasonal fiction and nonfiction.

LESSON: Meet in story corner.
  Check attendance. Cranberry—books returned
      Limes—books not returned

Review collages and photographs. Introduce and discuss watercolors and woodcuts. Show examples. Introduce story, read and discuss. Tell briefly of books on display.

BOOK SELECTION: Students return to story corner. Have students check their books for the type of illustrations. Review lesson. Dismiss.

Lesson 3

SKILL: Identifying different types of illustrations.

OBJECTIVE: Students will review collages and photographs, watercolors and woodcuts, and be introduced to tempera paint and pencil as mediums of illustrations.

LITERATURE: Books using tempera paint and pencil as illustrations.

PREPARATION: Make a copy of the terms "tempera paint" and "pencil." A copy of the terms "collages," "photographs," "watercolors," and "woodcuts." Display a selection of books using tempera paint and pencil, as well as seasonal fiction and nonfiction. Select one to use with the class.

LESSON: Meet in story corner.
Check attendance. Cranberry—books returned
Limes—books not returned

Review collages and photographs, watercolors and woodcuts. Introduce tempera paint and pencil, and discuss. Introduce story, read and discuss. Tell briefly of books on display.

BOOK SELECTION: Students return to story corner. Have students check their books for types of illustrations. Review lesson. Dismiss.

Lesson 4

SKILL: Identifying different mediums of illustrations.

OBJECTIVE: Students will practice identifying the six mediums of illustration.

LITERATURE: Seasonal fiction and nonfiction.

PREPARATION: Books using each medium at tables. A copy of each term. Display a selection of seasonal fiction and nonfiction. Select one to use with the class.

LESSON: Meet in story corner.
Check attendance. Cranberry—books returned
Limes—books not returned

Move to tables. Hold up a term. Students will determine which book or books contain that medium. Continue for all terms. Introduce story, read and discuss. Tell briefly of books on display.

BOOK SELECTION: Students return to story corner. Have students determine the type of illustration in their books. Review lesson. Dismiss.

INFORMATION SHEET:
ALL ABOUT ILLUSTRATIONS

Illustrators use their drawings to help tell a story to the audience. The visual image adds impact to the printed word as well as adding continuity from one page to the next.

The medium the illustrator chooses is very important. The medium affects how the illustrations look and can help create the feeling that the illustrator wants them to have.

Some examples of different mediums available to the illustrator are:

Collage	Watercolor	Photograph
Woodcut	Tempera paint	Pencil

1. *COLLAGE:* A method that involves cutting out and pasting down each shape to form the picture. The shapes are colored before being cut and assembled.

2. *WOODCUT:* A method that involves carving out a wood block with special tools. The wood that remains prints black when ink is rubbed over the block. The artist can then add colors to the black outlines that have been formed.

3. *WATERCOLOR:* Thin paints to which water is added. Special paper is used to help the colors blend together. Soft, pastel colors and smooth flowing shapes result.

4. *TEMPERA PAINT:* Bright, bold colors that dry fast characterize tempera paint. Strong, solid shapes that do not blend into each other result.

5. *PHOTOGRAPH:* True-to-life (real images) are reproduced on sensitive paper when it is exposed to light and chemical action. A photograph can be black and white or full color.

6. *PENCIL:* The side of colored pencils create light, soft shapes like watercolors, but do not blend together. The point of the pencil is used to add fine detail.

COMBINATION: Sometimes an illustrator uses two or more of the above mediums to help create the look he or she wants.

EXAMPLES OF MEDIUMS IN DIFFERENT STORIES

A fairy tale, for example, *Cinderella* by Marcia Brown, was rendered beautifully in watercolors for a delicate, soft look that helps convey the feeling of the story.

In contrast, in the *Stonecutter* by Gerald McDermott, a tempera paint/collage was used. The strong, bold tempera colors were cut up into strong, simple shapes. They helped to depict the strength of the mountain and the immensity of the stonecutter's task.

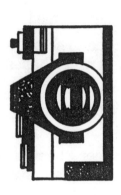

PHOTOGRAPH

(insert photographs)

COLLAGE

WATERCOLOR

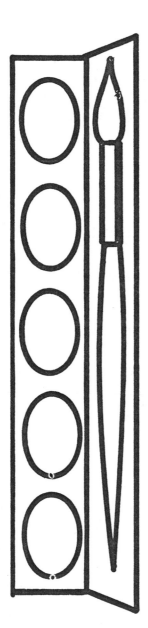

WOODCUT

TEMPERA PAINT

GREEN

BLUE

YELLOW

RED

PENCIL

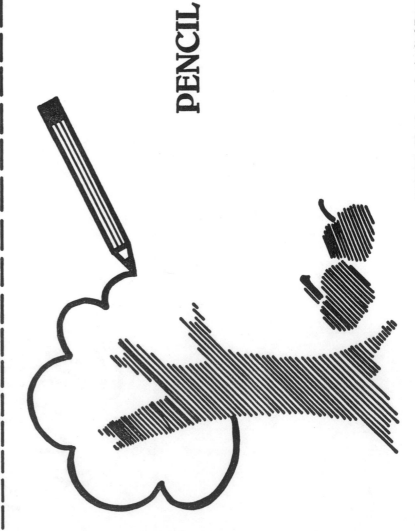

JANUARY

Lesson 1

SKILL: Appreciation of literature and illustrations.

OBJECTIVE: Students will be introduced to the Caldecott Award books.

LITERATURE: Caldecott Award books.

PREPARATION: This unit should be completed with one class at a time. Rotate if there are several sections. Plan unit with classroom teacher. Gather together the Caldecott collection, keeping out the ones to be used in the lessons, plus all media and materials pertaining to the collection. Sign out to the classroom. Display the honors collection for circulation. A copy of the list of winners for each student.

LESSON: Meet in story corner.
Check attendance. Gold Medal—books returned
Silver Medal—books not returned

Introduce and discuss Randolph Caldecott and the Caldecott Award. Explain how the unit will work. Introduce one title, read and discuss. Tell briefly of honors collection displayed.

BOOK SELECTION: Students return to story corner. Have students check copyright date in honors books. Tell what title won for that year. Review lesson. Dismiss.

Lesson 2

SKILL: Appreciation of literature and illustrations.

OBJECTIVE: Continuation of the Caldecott Award collection.

LITERATURE: Caldecott honors books.

PREPARATION: A Caldecott Award title. Display the honors collection.

LESSON: Meet in story corner.
Check attendance. Gold Medal—books returned
Silver Medal—books not returned

Discuss the titles read by students during the week. Introduce, read and discuss story. Tell briefly of books on display.

BOOK SELECTION: Students return to story corner. Have students check copyright date of honors books. Tell what title won the award for that year. Review lesson. Dismiss.

Lesson 3

SKILL: Appreciation of literature and illustrations.

OBJECTIVE: Continuation of the Caldecott Award.

LITERATURE: Caldecott honors books.

PREPARATION: A Caldecott title. Display the Caldecott honors collection. Vary the illustration medium to reinforce December's lessons.

LESSON: Meet in story corner.
Check attendance. Gold Medal—books returned
Silver Medal—books not returned

Discuss titles read by students during week. Discuss illustrations. Have students begin to think which title is their favorite. Explain they will illustrate their favorite next week. Introduce story, read and discuss. Tell briefly of books on display.

BOOK SELECTION: Students return to story corner. Review lesson. Dismiss.

Lesson 4

SKILL: Appreciation of literature and illustrations.

OBJECTIVE: Students will determine their favorite Caldecott winner title and complete an activity based on that title.

PREPARATION: A copy of the activity "My Favorite Caldecott Book" for each student. Crayons. Have all Caldecott materials returned from classroom. Display all titles for circulation.

LESSON: Meet in story corner.
Check attendance. Gold Medal—books returned
Silver Medal—books not returned

Move to tables. Hand out materials. Have students complete activity. Prepare a bulletin board in library or classroom using activity.

BOOK SELECTION: Students return to story corner. Discuss mediums of illustrations and the relationship of illustration to text. Review lesson and unit. Dismiss.

CALDECOTT GOLD MEDAL WINNERS

1938 Fish, Helen. *Animals of the Bible*. Illustrated by Dorothy Lathrop.

1939 Handforth, Thomas. *Mei Li*.

1940 d'Aulaire, Ingri and Edgar d'Aulaire. *Abraham Lincoln*.

1941 Lawson, Robert. *They Were Strong and Good*.

1942 McCloskey, Robert. *Make Way for Ducklings*.

1943 Burton, Virginia. *The Little House*.

1944 Thurber, James. *Many Moons*.

1945 Field, Rachel. *Prayer for a Child*.

1946 Petersham, Maud and Miska Petersham. *The Rooster Crows*.

1947 MacDonald, Golden. *The Little Island*.

1948 Tresselt, Alvin. *White Snow, Bright Snow*.

1949 Hader, Berta and Elmer Hader. *The Big Snow*.

1950 Politi, Leo. *Song of the Swallows*.

1951 Milhous, Katherine. *The Egg Tree*.

1952 Lipkind, William. *Finders Keepers*. Illustrated by Nicolas Mordinoff.

1953 Ward, Lynd. *The Biggest Bear*.

1954 Bemelmans, Ludwig. *Madeline's Rescue*.

1955 Perrault, Charles. *Cinderella*. Illustrated by Marcia Brown.

1956 Langstaff, John, ed. *Frog Went A-Courting*. Illustrated by Feodor Rojankovsky.

1957 Udry, Janice May. *A Tree is Nice*. Illustrated by Marc Simont.

1958 McCloskey, Robert. *Time of Wonder*.

1959 Chaucer, Geoffrey. *Chanticleer and the Fox*. Translated by Robert Mayer Lumiansky. Adapted and illustrated by Barbara Cooney.

1960 Ets, Marie Hall, and Aurora Labastida. *Nine Days to Christmas*. Illustrated by Marie Hall Ets.

1961 Robbins, Ruth. *Baboushka and the Three Kings*. Illustrated by Nicolas Sidjakov.

1962 Brown, Marcia. *Once a Mouse....*

1963 Keats, Ezra Jack. *The Snowy Day*.

1964 Sendak, Maurice. *Where the Wild Things Are*.

1965 de Regniers, Beatrice Schenk. *May I Bring a Friend*. Illustrated by Beni Montressor.

1966 Alger, Leclaire (Sorche Nic Leodhas) *Always Room for One More*. Illustrated by Nonny Hogrogian.

1967 Ness, Evaline. *Sam, Bangs and Moonshine*.

1968 Emberley, Barbara. *Drummer Hoff*. Illustrated by Ed Emberley.

1969 Ransome, Arthur. *The Fool of the World and the Flying Ship*. Illustrated by Uri Shulevitz.

1970 Steig, William. *Sylvester and the Magic Pebble*.

1971 Haley, Gail. *A Story, A Story: An African Tale*.

1972 Hogrogian, Nonny. *One Fine Day*.

1973 Mosel, Arlene. *The Funny Little Woman*.

1974 Zemach, Harve. *Duffy and the Devil*. Illustrated by Margot Zemach.

CALDECOTT GOLD MEDAL WINNERS (continued)

1975 McDermott, Gerald. *Arrow to the Sun.*

1976 Aardema, Verna. *Why Mosquitos Buzz in People's Ears.* Illustrated by Leo and Diane Dillon.

1977 Musgrove, Margaret. *Ashanti to Zulu.* Illustrated by Leo and Diane Dillon.

1978 Spier, Peter. *Noah's Ark.*

1979 Gobel, Paul. *The Girl Who Loved Wild Horses.*

1980 Hall, Donald. *Ox-Cart Man.* Illustrated by Barbara Cooney.

1981 Lobel, Arnold. *Fables.*

1982 Van Allsburg, Chris. Jumanji.

1983 Cendrars, Blaise. *Shadow.* Translated and illustrated by Marcia Brown.

1984 Provensen, Alice and Martin. *The Glorious Flight.*

1985 Hodges, Margaret. *Saint George and the Dragon.* Illustrated by Trina Schart Hyman.

1986 Van Allsburg, Chris. *The Polar Express.*

1987 Yorinks, Arthur. *Hey, Al.* Illustrated by Richard Egielski.

Name _____   Date _____

MY FAVORITE CALDECOTT BOOK

DIRECTIONS: Draw an example of the illustrations that appear in your favorite Caldecott Award book. Then complete the information below.

AUTHOR _____

TITLE _____

YEAR_____

MEDIUM OF ILLUSTRATION _____

FEBRUARY

Lesson 1

SKILL: Knowledge and understanding of biography.

OBJECTIVE: Students will be introduced to biography as a type of nonfiction and how biography is shelved.

LITERATURE: Biography.

PREPARATION: A copy of the term "biography." Select 4 to 5 biographies for class use. Display a selection of biography. Select one to use with the class.

LESSON: Meet in story corner.
Check attendance. Cherries—books returned
Grapes—books not returned

Introduce biography and the call number used in your collection. Discuss why biography is shelved by subject rather than author. Show selected titles. Move to biography shelves if possible. Have students give names of famous persons. Show where shelved. Return to story corner. Introduce biography, read and discuss. Tell briefly of books on display.

BOOK SELECTION: Students return to story corner. Have students check spine for call number. Review lesson. Dismiss.

Lesson 2

SKILL: Knowledge and understanding of biography and autobiography.

OBJECTIVE: Students will review their knowledge of biography and be introduced to autobiography.

LITERATURE: Biography and autobiography.

PREPARATION: A copy of the terms biography and autobiography. Display a selection of biographies and autobiographies. Select one to use with the class.

LESSON: Meet in story corner.
Check attendance. Cherries—books returned
Grapes—books not returned

> Review biography. Introduce and discuss autobiography. Discuss the differences in call number. Introduce biography, read and discuss. Tell briefly of books on display.
>
> *BOOK SELECTION:* Students return to story corner. Review lesson. Dismiss.

Lesson 3

SKILL: Knowledge and understanding of biography, autobiography, and collective biography.

OBJECTIVE: Students will review and reinforce their knowledge of biography and autobiography. Students will be introduced to collective biography.

LITERATURE: Biography, autobiography, and collective biography.

PREPARATION: A copy of the terms biography, autobiography, and collective biography. Select examples of biography, autobiography, and collective biography. Display a selection of all three. Select one title to use with the class.

> *LESSON:* Meet in story corner.
> Check attendance. Cherries—books returned
> Grapes—books not returned
>
> Review biography and autobiography. Introduce collective biography. Explain call number. Using selected books, give a synopsis of each. Have students decide which is biography, autobiography, or collective biography. Introduce title, read and discuss. Tell briefly of books on display.
>
> *BOOK SELECTION:* Students return to story corner. Review lesson. Dismiss.

Lesson 4

SKILL: Knowledge and understanding of biography, autobiography, and collective biography.

OBJECTIVE: Students will complete an activity designed to assess their knowledge of the three kinds of biography.

LITERATURE: Biography, autobiography, and collective biography.

PREPARATION: A copy of the activity "Biography, Autobiography, or Collective Biography?" for each student. Make a transparency for introduction. Overhead projector. Display a selection of the three kinds of biography. Select one to use with the class if time allows.

LESSON: Meet in story corner.
Check attendance. Cherries—books returned
Grapes—books not returned

Move to tables. Hand out materials. Using transparency, introduce activity. Have students complete activity. Correct together. If there is time, move to story corner. Introduce title, read and discuss. Tell briefly of books on display.

BOOK SELECTION: Students return to story corner. Review unit. Dismiss.

BIOGRAPHY, AUTOBIOGRAPHY, OR COLLECTIVE BIOGRAPHY?

DIRECTIONS: Decide whether the books below are biography, autobiography, or collective biography. Circle the correct answer below each and write the correct call number on each spine.

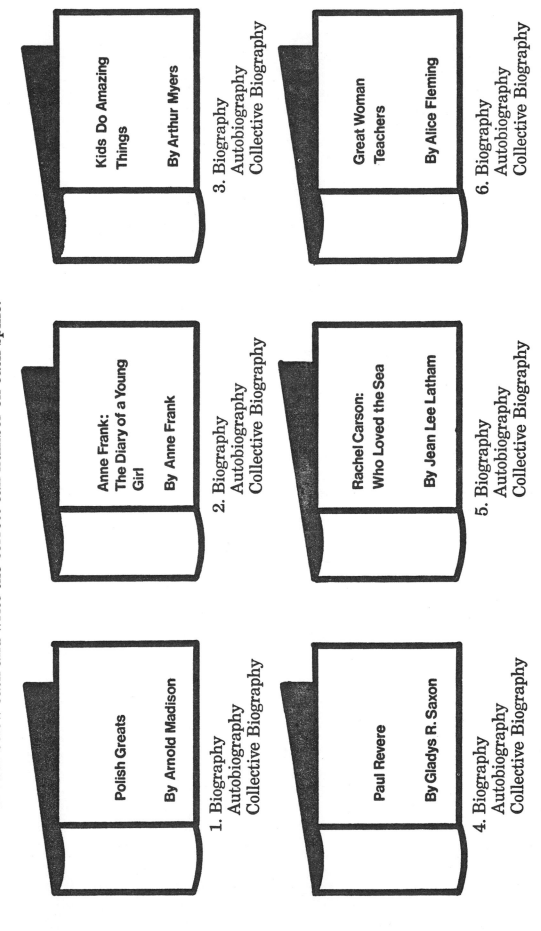

Polish Greats

By Arnold Madison

1. Biography
   Autobiography
   Collective Biography

Anne Frank:
The Diary of a Young
Girl

By Anne Frank

2. Biography
   Autobiography
   Collective Biography

Kids Do Amazing
Things

By Arthur Myers

3. Biography
   Autobiography
   Collective Biography

Paul Revere

By Gladys R. Saxon

4. Biography
   Autobiography
   Collective Biography

Rachel Carson:
Who Loved the Sea

By Jean Lee Latham

5. Biography
   Autobiography
   Collective Biography

Great Woman
Teachers

By Alice Fleming

6. Biography
   Autobiography
   Collective Biography

MARCH

Lesson 1

SKILL: Knowledge and understanding of the Dewey Decimal System and the relationship of the call number.

OBJECTIVE: Students will be introduced to the arrangement of nonfiction and the Dewey Decimal System. Students will be introduced to the 100s, the 200s, and the 300s.

LITERATURE: Nonfiction from the 100s, the 200s, and the 300s.

PREPARATION: A copy of the Dewey Decimal System. Gather together materials for introducing and teaching the system. Display a selection of books from the 100s, the 200s, and the 300s. Select one to use with the class.

LESSON: If possible, meet in front of the 100s to 300s. If not, meet in story corner. Check attendance. Strawberries—books returned
Lemons—books not returned

Introduce and discuss the Dewey Decimal System. Introduce the 100s to 300s. Introduce title, read and discuss. Tell briefly of books on display.

BOOK SELECTION: Students return to story corner. Review lesson. Dismiss.

Lesson 2

SKILL: Knowledge and understanding of the Dewey Decimal System.

OBJECTIVE: Students will review the 100s to 300s. Students will be introduced to the 400s to 600s.

LITERATURE: Nonfiction from the 400s, the 500s, and the 600s.

PREPARATION: A copy of the Dewey main classes. Display a selection of 400s to 600s. Select one to use with the class.

LESSON: Meet in front of the 400s to 600s shelving if possible. If not, meet in story corner.
Check attendance. Strawberries—books returned
Lemons—books not returned

Review the 100s to 300s. Introduce the 400s to 600s. Introduce title, read and discuss. Tell briefly of books on display.

> *BOOK SELECTION:* Students return to story corner. Have students check the spines of their books for call number. Review lesson. Dismiss.

Lesson 3

SKILL: Knowledge and understanding of the Dewey Decimal System.

OBJECTIVE: Students will review the 100s to 600s. Students will be introduced to the 700s to 900s.

LITERATURE: Nonfiction from the 700s to 900s.

PREPARATION: A copy of the Dewey main classes. Display a selection of books from the 700s to 900s. Select one to use with the class.

> *LESSON:* Meet in front of the 700s to 900s if possible. If not, meet in story corner. Check attendance. Strawberries—books returned
> Lemons—books not returned
>
> Review the 100s to 600s. Introduce the 700s to 900s. Introduce title, read and discuss. Tell briefly of books on display.
>
> *BOOK SELECTION:* Students return to story corner. Have students check the spines of their books for call number. Review lesson. Dismiss.

Lesson 4

SKILL: Knowledge and understanding of the Dewey Decimal System.

OBJECTIVE: Students will review the 100s to 900s. Students will be introduced to the 000s. Display a selection of nonfiction. Select one to use with the class or use a filmstrip for review.

LITERATURE: Nonfiction selections.

PREPARATION: A copy of the main classes. Display a selection of nonfiction. Select a 000 to use with the class.

> *LESSON:* Meet in front of the 000s shelving if possible. If not, meet in story corner.
> Check attendance. Strawberries—books returned
> Lemons—books not returned
>
> Review 100s to 900s. Introduce 000s. Discuss reference materials. Introduce title, read and discuss. Tell briefly of books on display.

BOOK SELECTION: Students return to story corner. Review the Dewey Decimal System. Dismiss.

APRIL

Lesson 1

SKILL: Review and reinforcement of characters, main characters, and supporting characters.

OBJECTIVE: Students will review and reinforce the above concepts through a unit on the American tall tales.

LITERATURE: Tall tales.

PREPARATION: This unit is most successful when correlated with the classroom. Gather together all print and nonprint materials, saving three to use in lessons in the library. Sign out to the classroom. Make a transparency of the map of the United States for a bulletin board in the classroom. Select a tall tale to use with the class.

LESSON: Meet in story corner.
        Check attendance. Watermelon—books returned
                Apricots—books not returned

Introduce the tall tales. Compare with fairy tales. Explain that students will immerse themselves in tall tales for a month and will choose their favorite character. Introduce story, read and discuss. Tell briefly of books on display.

BOOK SELECTION: Students return to story corner. Review lesson. Dismiss.

Lesson 2

SKILL: Review and reinforcement of characters, main character, and supporting characters.

OBJECTIVE: Students will review and reinforce the above concepts through a unit on the American tall tales.

LITERATURE: Tall tales. Classic folk and fairy tales for comparison to the American tall tales.

PREPARATION: A tall tale to use with the class. Display a selection of classic folk and fairy tales.

> *LESSON:* Meet in story corner.
> Check attendance. Watermelon—books returned
> Apricots—books not returned
>
> Review main character and supporting characters. Compare the elements in a fairy tale and the elements in the tall tales. Invite students to tell about the tall tale characters they have met during the week. Introduce story, read and discuss. Tell briefly of books on display.
>
> *BOOK SELECTION:* Students return to story corner. Review lesson. Dismiss.

Lesson 3

SKILL: Review and reinforcement of setting.

OBJECTIVE: Students will review and reinforce the concept of setting through a unit on the American tall tales.

LITERATURE: American tall tales. Classic folk and fairy tales.

PREPARATION: A tall tale to use with the class. Display a selection of classic folk and fairy tales.

> *LESSON:* Meet in story corner.
> Check attendance. Watermelon—books returned
> Apricots—books not returned
>
> Discuss the elements of a tall tale versus the elements of a fairy tale. Discuss the tall tales read during the week in the classroom. Discuss the setting of the tall tales, and why setting is so important (historical aspect). Introduce tall tale, read and discuss. Tell briefly of books on display.
>
> *BOOK SELECTION:* Students return to story corner. Review lesson. Explain that students are to choose their favorite tall tale character during the week.

Lesson 4

SKILL: Review of characters and setting.

OBJECTIVE: Students will illustrate the main character and setting of their favorite tall tale.

LITERATURE: American tall tales.

PREPARATION: A copy of the activity "My Favorite Tall Tale Character" for each student. Crayons. Make a transparency of activity for introduction of activity. Overhead projector. Bring back materials from classroom. Display for circulation.

LESSON: Meet in story corner.
    Check attendance. Watermelon—books returned
            Apricots—books not returned

Discuss all tall tale characters. Move to tables. Hand out materials. Using transparency, introduce activity. Have students complete activity. Drawings should be displayed in library or classroom. Tell briefly of books on display.

BOOK SELECTION: Students return to story corner. Review unit. Dismiss.

© 1988 by The Center for Applied Research in Education

MAP OF THE UNITED STATES

Name _____   Date _____

MY FAVORITE TALL TALE CHARACTER

DIRECTIONS: Draw a picture of your favorite tall tale character in action. Then complete the information below.

CHARACTER _____

SUPPORTING CHARACTERS _____

SETTING _____

TELL ABOUT THE CHARACTER _____

_____

_____

_____

MAY

Lesson 1

SKILL: Knowledge and understanding of the fiction section of the library.

OBJECTIVE: Students will be introduced to the fiction section of the library.

LITERATURE: Easier fiction.

PREPARATION: A copy of the terms fiction and nonfiction. Display books in a series by Haywood, Cleary, or Chew. Choose one from which to read the first chapter, or a filmstrip of one of the books.

LESSON: Meet in story corner.
Check attendance. Plums—books returned
Cantaloupe—books not returned

Review fiction and nonfiction. Demonstrate how fiction is shelved. Introduce author. Read first chapter or show filmstrip and discuss. Tell briefly of books on display.

LESSON: Students return to story corner. Review lesson. Dismiss.

Lesson 2

SKILL: Knowledge and understanding of the fiction section of the library.

OBJECTIVE: Students will become familiar with the fiction section.

LITERATURE: Appropriate fiction books in a series.

PREPARATION: Gather together all print and nonprint materials by one author. Plan with classroom teacher to have the audio visual material shown or book read in the classroom. Prepare a brief talk on the biography of the author and a book talk on the books. Display all titles.

LESSON: Meet in story corner.
Check attendance. Plums—books returned
Cantaloupe—books not returned

Review fiction. Review author introduced last week. Show where books are shelved. Introduce today's author and show where books are shelved. Give talk and discuss.

BOOK SELECTION: Students return to story corner. Have students check the call number of their books. How many fiction? How many nonfiction? Review lesson. Dismiss.

Lesson 3

SKILL: Knowledge and understanding of the fiction section of the library.

OBJECTIVE: Students will be introduced to appropriate fiction authors.

LITERATURE: Fiction by appropriate authors.

PREPARATION: Gather together fiction by several authors. Prepare a book talk.

LESSON: Meet in front of fiction shelves if possible, or meet in story corner. Check attendance. Plums—books returned
Cantaloupe—books not returned

Review fiction. Review authors previously introduced. Give book talk.

BOOK SELECTION: Students return to fiction section or story corner. Review lesson. Dismiss.

Lesson 4

SKILL: Knowledge and understanding of fiction and the arrangement of fiction on the shelf.

OBJECTIVE: Students will review appropriate authors and be introduced to the arrangement of fiction on the shelf.

LITERATURE: Appropriate fiction.

PREPARATION: Display appropriate fiction.

LESSON: Meet students at the door. Have students returning fiction books bring the books with them. Meet in front of fiction shelves.
Check attendance. Plums—books returned
Cantaloupe—books not returned

Have students with fiction books, in turn, show book, tell author and title, and give a brief synopsis of the book. Demonstrate where the book would be shelved and why. Collect the books to be carded and displayed for circulation. Tell briefly of other books on display.

BOOK SELECTION: Students return to fiction shelves. Review unit. Dismiss.

JUNE

Lesson 1

SKILL: Knowledge and use of magazines.

OBJECTIVE: Students will be introduced to the magazine titles available in the library.

LITERATURE: Magazines.

PREPARATION: Gather together all appropriate magazine titles. Have at least one issue of each title on each table. Make enough copies of activity "Magazines" for each student to have one copy of activity for each title. A transparency of activity for introduction. Overhead projector. Make a transparency listing titles of magazines.

LESSON: Meet in story corner.
Check attendance. Peaches—books returned
Tangerines—books not returned

Have students move to tables. Hand out activity. Using transparency, introduce activity. Students are to browse through each magazine title and complete a sheet for each. This activity will continue next week. Collect activity sheets to be returned next week.

BOOK SELECTION: Students return to story corner. Review lesson. Dismiss.

Lesson 2

SKILL: Knowledge and use of magazines.

OBJECTIVE: Students will become familiar with the contents of the magazine titles available in the library.

LITERATURE: Magazines.

PREPARATION: Magazine titles on tables. Activity sheets. List of magazine titles available.

LESSON: Students meet in story corner.
Check attendance. Peaches—books returned
Tangerines—books not returned

Have students move to tables. Complete activity started last week.

BOOK SELECTION: Students return to story corner. Review lesson. Students will illustrate a cover for their favorite magazine next week.

Lesson 3

SKILL: Knowledge and use of magazines.

OBJECTIVE: Students will select their favorite magazine title and design a cover for that magazine.

LITERATURE: Magazines.

PREPARATION: A copy of the activity "My Favorite Magazine" for each student. Crayons. Issues of each magazine title.

LESSON: Meet in story corner.
Check attendance. Peaches—books returned
Tangerines—books not returned

Have students move to tables. Introduce activity. Have students complete activity.

BOOK SELECTION: Students return to story corner. Review lesson. Dismiss.

Lesson 4

SKILL: Recall of authors and titles.

OBJECTIVE: Students will recall authors and titles of books read during the year.

PREPARATION: Display board. Large sheets of paper. Felt marker. Label one sheet *Authors,* another sheet *Titles,* a third sheet, *A GOOD PLACE TO READ*..... Have extra sheets of paper.

LESSON: Meet in story corner.
Check attendance. Peaches—books returned
Tangerines—books not returned

Using large sheet labeled *Authors,* have students think of all authors' names they know. List them on the sheet. Then, list all titles students can remember. If there is time, make a list of good places to read this summer. Discuss any summer reading programs available. Review skills covered during the year. Dismiss.

Name _____   Date _____

MAGAZINES

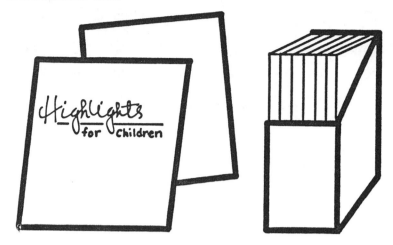

Title of magazine _____

Month and year of magazine _____

Study the magazine, checking what the magazine offers. Answer the following questions.

1. Does the magazine have fiction stories? Yes _____ No _____

2. Does the magazine have nonfiction articles? Yes _____ No _____

3. Does the magazine have illustrations? Yes _____ No _____

4. Does the magazine have puzzles? Yes _____ No _____

5. Does the magazine have games? Yes _____ No _____

6. How often is the magazine published? Monthly_____ Bimonthly _____

7. How much does the magazine cost for a subscription?_____

8. Would the magazine help you with your school work or is it mainly for recreational reading?

   _____

   _____

   _____

9. What is your opinion of the magazine and why? _____

   _____

   _____

   _____

Name _____   Date _____

MY FAVORITE MAGAZINE

DIRECTIONS: Draw a monthly cover for your favorite magazine. Include title, month, and year. Use the same format as the magazine.

I like _____ because _____

_____

_____

_____

_____

GRADE 3

OVERVIEW

The main objectives in third grade are:

- to have students demonstrate mastery of the terms, concepts, and skills introduced, reviewed, and reinforced in kindergarten through second grade.
- to continue to introduce parts of the book.
- to introduce and teach card catalog skills.
- to introduce and teach encyclopedia skills.
- to introduce the atlas.
- to introduce different genres to further develop students' interest areas.

Terms and Concepts To Be Mastered

Regulations and procedures of the facility.

Author, Title, Illustrator, Illustrations, Publisher, Place of Publication, Copyright, Copyright Date.

Spine, Cover, Pages, Dust Jacket, Dedication Page, Title Page, Copyright Page.

Main Character, Supporting Characters, Setting, Plot.

Parts of a story: Beginning, Middle, End.

Terms, Concepts, and Skills To Be Introduced or Reinforced

Table of Contents, Index

Alphabetizing

Arrangement of fiction and nonfiction

Card Catalog Skills:

   Catalog Cards; Author, Title, Subject

   Outside Guides of Card Catalog

   Information on catalog cards

   Locating material on shelves

Biography

Encyclopedias:

   Locating proper volume: single and split letter

   Locating key words

Locating information
Atlas:
   Physical and Political maps
   Location skills

Literature: Monthly Genre

Fables   Seasonal
Historical   Science Fiction
Mystery and Detective   Family and School
Animals   Adventure
Biography   Humorous Poetry
Humorous   Fantasy

Special Notes

1. Beginning in third grade, a library folder should be used for each student to keep his or her work intact throughout the year. The folders may consist of oaktag or construction paper. The student's name should be on the cover, which can be illustrated in correlation with art classes or illustrated in the library. Keep the folders in the library. They should be placed on the tables just prior to the arrival of the class and collected at the end of the class.

2. If tables are used for seating, use assigned seating. Assign a mixture of students with strong skills background and students with weaker skills background for a working group. A large percentage of the skill work will be completed in table units working together. If table groups are large, consisting of eight or more students each, divide into two groups within the main group. Give each table a number. Divide the folders into table groups, with a 4 × 6-inch sheet of paper or construction paper with the number of table and names of students in the group. This will separate the folders, making distribution and collection quick and easy.

3. Beginning in third grade, a curriculum of formal library skills should be initiated. There is less time for reading to students, but you can begin to select short stories from anthologies. Reading chapters from books is not recommended due to the time lapse between meetings. A chapter book may take up to six weeks to complete and many students may find it difficult to sustain interest for that length of time. The classroom teachers should be encouraged to read daily to the students, however. Recommending authors and titles to the classroom teachers should help achieve results.

4. Filmstrips and other media adaptations can be used successfully to introduce an author, a title, a series of titles, or literature genre. The first

lesson of each month, when a different genre is introduced, is a good time for a filmstrip or other media. Another good time is for a change of pace between units or particular skills.

SEPTEMBER

Lesson 1

SKILL: Knowledge of library regulations. Knowledge and understanding of the sections of the library.

OBJECTIVE: Students will review library regulations. Students will review the sections of the library.

LITERATURE: Family and school fiction and nonfiction.

PREPARATION: A copy of the activity "Treasure Hunt in _____" for each student. Crayons. A transparency of activity. Overhead projector. A folder for each student. A piece of 4 × 6-inch paper for table number. Class roster. Display family and school fiction and nonfiction.

LESSON: Students sit where they wish. Check attendance. Hand out materials. Using transparency, complete activity with class, coloring each square after reviewing section. Review library procedures and regulations. Tell briefly of books on display.

BOOK SELECTION: Students return to tables. Review lesson. Students put folders in middle of table with table number sheet on top. Dismiss by tables. Collect folders.

Lesson 2

SKILL: Review of concepts.

OBJECTIVE: Students will review the concepts of author, title, illustrator, illustrations, publisher, place of publication, copyright date, and call number.

LITERATURE: Family and school fiction and nonfiction.

PREPARATION: A copy of the activity "The Business of Books" for each student. Transparency of activity. Overhead projector. Permanent seating plan. Display family and school fiction and nonfiction. Folders to be passed out.

> *LESSON:* Assign seating. Pass out folders. Hand out activity sheets. Using transparency, introduce, and complete activity with class. Tell briefly of books on display.
>
> *BOOK SELECTION:* Students return to tables. Review lesson. Students put folders in middle on table with table number on top. Dismiss by tables. Collect folders.

Lesson 3

SKILL: Review of parts of the book.

OBJECTIVE: Students will review the spine, cover, pages, dust jacket, dedication page, and copyright page.

LITERATURE: Family and school fiction and nonfiction.

PREPARATION: A copy of the activity "What Part of the Book Am I?" for each student. A transparency of activity. Overhead projector. Display family and school fiction and nonfiction. Place folders on tables.

> *LESSON:* Students take assigned seats. Check attendance. Hand out activity. Using transparency, introduce activity. Students complete activity. Correct together, using transparency. Tell briefly of books on display.
>
> *BOOK SELECTION:* Students return to tables. Review lesson. Dismiss by tables. Collect folders.

Lesson 4

SKILL: Review of sections of a story and elements of a story.

OBJECTIVE: Students will review the sections of a story and the elements of a story.

LITERATURE: Family and school fiction and nonfiction.

PREPARATION: A copy of the activity "It's All Part of the Story" for each student. A transparency of activity. Overhead projector. Display family and school fiction and nonfiction. Place folders on tables.

> *LESSON:* Students take assigned seats. Check attendance. Hand out activity. Using transparency, introduce activity. Students complete activity. Correct together, using transparency. Tell briefly of books on display.
>
> *BOOK SELECTION:* Students return to tables. Review lesson. Dismiss by tables. Collect folders.

Name _____ Date _____

TREASURE HUNT IN _____

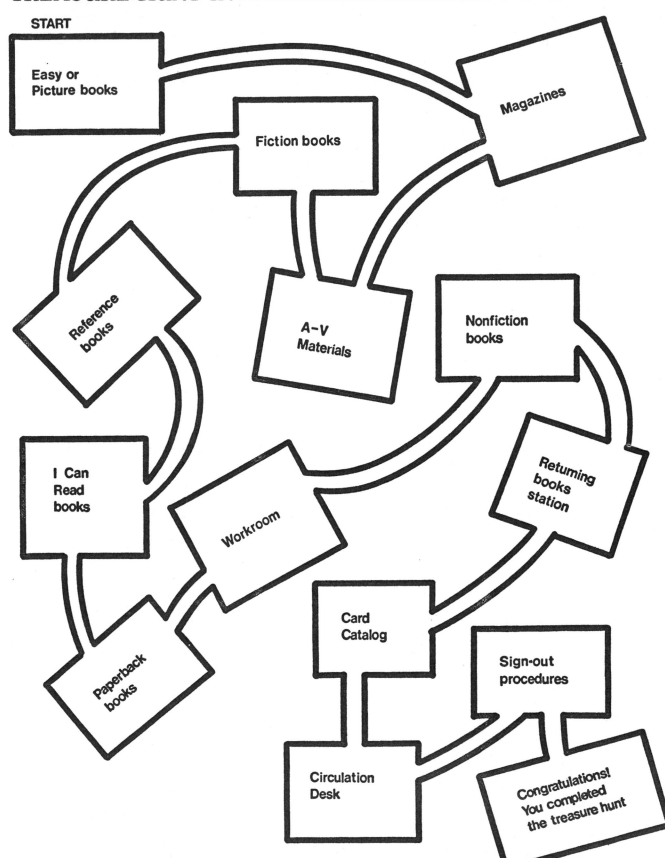

START

Easy or Picture books

Fiction books

Magazines

Reference books

A–V Materials

Nonfiction books

I Can Read books

Workroom

Returning books station

Paperback books

Card Catalog

Sign-out procedures

Circulation Desk

Congratulations! You completed the treasure hunt

Name _____   Date _____

THE BUSINESS OF BOOKS

ACROSS

4. The date the book is published is called the _____ date.
6. The name of the book is called the _____.
7. A person who writes a book is called the _____.
8. The drawings found in a book are called the _____.

DOWN

1. A person or company that prints and distributes printed material is called a _____.
2. The artist who creates the drawings in a book is called the _____.
3. The classification number and letter that identifies the subject and author is called the _____ _____.
5. Where the book is published is called the _____ _____ publication.

WORD BOX
AUTHOR, TITLE, ILLUSTRATOR, COPYRIGHT, ILLUSTRATIONS, PUBLISHER, CALL NUMBER, PLACE OF

Name _____   Date _____

WHAT PART
OF THE BOOK AM I?

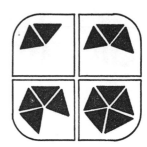

DIRECTIONS: Write the part of the book on the blank line.

1. I hold the book together and keep the book from bending. I am also called the backbone of the book. I have the call number printed on me.

   I am the _____ of the book.

2. I protect the pages. Part of me is called the front and part of me is called the back. I join the backbone of the book.

   I am the _____ of the book.

3. I and many others like me are the paper on which the story and pictures appear. There can be hundreds of us or just a few.

   We are the _____ of the book.

4. I help keep the cover clean and crisp. I am very attractive and add color to the book. I help you decide what book to borrow.

   I am the _____ of the book.

5. I am a special page in the book. My author uses me to thank someone special who helped in some way with the book.

   I am the _____ page.

6. I am very important. If you want to know when my book was published, you check my page.

   I am the _____ page.

IT'S ALL PART OF THIS STORY

DIRECTIONS: Complete the following information.

1. There are three parts to every story. Name the three parts in order.

   a. _____

   b. _____

   c. _____

2. Whoever is in a story is called a character. The most important character is called the _____ character.

3. Other characters who are important, but not the most important, are called the _____ characters.

4. Where the story takes place is called the _____.

5. The plan of events or what happens in the story is called the_____.

OCTOBER

Lesson 1

SKILL: Knowledge and understanding of the concepts.

OBJECTIVE: Students will demonstrate mastery of the concepts through a written test.

LITERATURE: Mystery and detective fiction and nonfiction.

PREPARATION: A copy of the test "Library Terms" for each student. A transparency for directions. Overhead projector. Display mystery and detective fiction and nonfiction. Materials to introduce genre. Place folders on tables.

LESSON: Students take assigned seats. Check attendance. Hand out test. Using transparency, introduce test. Students complete test. Collect to correct. Complete test on transparency. Introduce genre. Tell briefly of books on display.

BOOK SELECTION: Students return to tables. Review lesson. Dismiss by tables. Collect folders.

Lesson 2

SKILL: Knowledge and understanding of the parts of the book.

OBJECTIVE: Students will demonstrate mastery of the parts of the book through a written test.

LITERATURE: Mystery and detective fiction and nonfiction.

PREPARATION: A copy of the test "Parts of the Book" for each student. A transparency of the activity. Overhead projector. Display mystery and detective fiction. Place folders on tables.

LESSON: Students take assigned seats. Check attendance. Hand out test. Using transparency, introduce test. Students complete test. Collect to correct. Complete test on transparency. Tell briefly of books on display.

BOOK SELECTION: Students return to tables. Review lesson. Dismiss by tables. Collect folders.

Lesson 3

SKILL: Knowledge and understanding of the elements of a story.

OBJECTIVE: Students will demonstrate mastery of the elements of a story through a written test.

LITERATURE: Mystery and detective fiction and nonfiction.

PREPARATION: A copy of the test "The Secret of Sandwich Island" for each student. A transparency for directions. Overhead projector. Display mystery and detective fiction and nonfiction. Place folders on tables.

LESSON: Students take assigned seats. Check attendance. Hand out test. Using transparency, introduce test. Students complete test. Collect to correct. Complete test on transparency. Tell briefly of books on display.

BOOK SELECTION: Students return to tables. Review lesson. Dismiss by tables. Collect folders.

Lesson 4

SKILL: Knowledge and understanding of hardware and software.

OBJECTIVE: Students will demonstrate mastery of the terms for the hardware and software available in the building.

LITERATURE: Mystery and detective fiction and nonfiction.

PREPARATION: Gather together one of each type of hardware and software available in the building. Arrange on a table. Display mystery and detective fiction and nonfiction. Place folders on tables.

LESSON: Students take assigned seats. Check attendance. Have a student go to table, hold up (or point out) a particular piece of hardware. Student calls on a table to name the hardware and what software goes with it. Repeat procedure. Tell briefly of books on display.

BOOK SELECTION: Students return to tables. Review lesson. Dismiss by tables. Collect folders.

Name _____   Date _____

LIBRARY TERMS

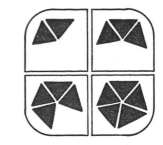

PART ONE
DIRECTIONS: Below are the definitions for library terms that you have learned. Write the name of the term on the line.

1. _____: The company that prints and sells the book.

2. _____: The artist that creates the pictures.

3. _____: The date the book is published or printed.

4. _____: Where the publisher is located.

5. _____: The person who writes the book.

6. _____: The pictures or drawings in the book.

7. _____: The name of the book.

8. _____: The right to copy for publication or to sell, any part or all of a printed work.

Encyclopedia Brown's 3rd Record Book of Weird & Wonderful Facts
By Donald J. Sobol Illustrated by Sal Murdocca William Morrow and Company New York 1985

PART TWO
DIRECTIONS: Use the information in the box at the left to complete the lines below.

Author _____

Title _____

_____

_____

Illustrator _____

Publisher _____

Copyright Date _____

Place of Publication _____

THE SECRET OF SANDWICH ISLAND

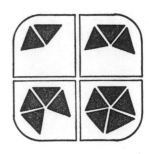

1. "Sir Hubert, you have failed twice." King Oswald pounded on the arm of the throne. "You have one last chance. Find the secret or I'll throw you into the dungeon."

2. King Oswald and Queen Flossie spend a good part of every day walking around Pancake Island, chatting with the people. They found out people cannot be ordered to be happy. Happiness comes from within, and now that King Oswald and Queen Flossie are happy, the people are happy too.

3. "Find the secret, Sir Hubert," King Oswald roared. Sir Hubert pulled his head into his brown cloak like a turtle. "Yes, Your Majesty," he gulped, as he tiptoed backwards out of the room. "Now, Dear," soothed Queen Flossie. "Try not to lose your temper." "Lose my temper!" King Oswald pounded the arm of the throne. "I lost my temper a long time ago. I must know the secret. I must know why Sandwich Island is such a happy place while our Pancake Island is not."

DIRECTIONS:

Answer the following questions.

Which of the above paragraphs would be found in the beginning, in the middle, and in the end of the story?

1. Beginning _____

   Middle _____

   End _____

2. Who is the main character? _____

3. Who are the supporting characters? _____

   _____

4. What is the setting of the story? _____

Name _____   Date _____

PARTS
OF THE BOOK

DIRECTIONS: Below are the definitions for the parts of the book that you have learned. Write the name of the part of the book on the line.

1. _____: The front and back boards that bind the book to the spine and protect the pages.

2. _____: The papers on which the story is printed.

3. _____: The backbone of the book.

4. _____: The protective cover for a book.

5. _____: The business page of the book, which includes the author, title, illustrator, publisher, and place of publication.

6. _____: The page on which the copyright date usually appears.

7. _____: The date the book is published.

8. _____: The page on which the author may thank someone in appreciation.

NOVEMBER

Lesson 1

SKILL: Knowledge and understanding of the table of contents and chapters.

OBJECTIVE: Students will be introduced to the table of contents.

LITERATURE: Historical fiction and nonfiction.

PREPARATION: Photocopy the table of contents from 4 to 5 books. Make transparencies. Overhead projector. Prepare introduction to historical fiction and nonfiction. Display historical fiction and nonfiction. Place folders on tables.

LESSON: Students take assigned seats. Check attendance. Introduce table of contents. Practice using table of contents. Introduce genre. Tell briefly of books on display.

BOOK SELECTION: Students return to tables. Review lesson. Dismiss by tables. Collect folders.

Lesson 2

SKILL: Knowledge and understanding of the table of contents and chapters.

OBJECTIVE: Students will complete an activity based on the table of contents.

LITERATURE: Historical fiction and nonfiction.

PREPARATION: A copy of the activity "The Table of Contents" for each student. A transparency of activity for introduction. Overhead projector. Display historical fiction and nonfiction. Place folders on tables.

LESSON: Students take assigned seats. Check attendance. Review table of contents. Hand out activity. Have students complete activity. Collect to correct. Complete activity on transparency with class. Tell briefly of books on display.

BOOK SELECTION: Students return to tables. Review lesson. Dismiss by tables. Collect folders.

Lesson 3

SKILL: Knowledge and understanding of the index.

OBJECTIVE: Students will be introduced to the index of the book.

LITERATURE: Historical fiction and nonfiction.

PREPARATION: Make a photocopy, then a transparency of the index from 4 to 5 books, citing use of comma and dash. Overhead projector. Display historical fiction and nonfiction. Place folders on tables.

LESSON: Students take assigned seats. Check attendance. Introduce index. Compare table of contents and index. Using transparencies, practice using an index. Tell briefly of books on display.

BOOK SELECTION: Students return to tables. Review lesson. Dismiss by tables. Collect folders.

Lesson 4

SKILL: Knowledge and understanding of the index.

OBJECTIVE: Students will complete an activity based on the index.

LITERATURE: Historical fiction and nonfiction.

PREPARATION: A copy of the activity "The Index of a Book" for each student. A transparency of activity for introduction. Display historical fiction and nonfiction. Place folders on tables.

LESSON: Students take assigned seats. Check attendance. Review index. Hand out activity. Introduce activity using transparency. Have students complete activity. Collect to correct. Complete activity on transparency with class. Tell briefly of books on display.

BOOK SELECTION: Students return to tables. Review tables of contents and index. Dismiss by tables. Collect folders.

THE TABLE OF CONTENTS

The word *contents* can be defined as all that something contains. It can be the contents of a box, the contents of a drawer, or the contents of a book. The contents of a book are divided into sections called *chapters* and special sections such as the introduction and the index.

The *TABLE OF CONTENTS* tells the chapter titles if there are any, the number of chapters, and the page on which each chapter begins.

DIRECTIONS: Use this sample table of contents to fill in the blanks at the bottom of this sheet.

CONTENTS

1. Birds	1
2. Animals	4
3. Insects	8
4. Flowers	12
5. Rocks and Minerals	20
6. Fruits	30
7. Oceans	34
8. Islands	41
9. Mountains	46
10. Planets	61
11. Fish	63
12. Deserts	74
13. Chemicals	80
14. Lakes	89
15. Rivers	100
Index	110

1. The chapter on *Oceans* is chapter number _____.

2. The chapter on *Deserts* begins on page _____.

3. The first chapter of the book is titled _____.

4. The chapter on *Mountains* contains _____ pages.

5. Chapter 9 is titled _____.

6. What chapter begins on page 30? _____.

7. Chapter _____ has the least number of pages.

8. The chapter on *Animals* contains _____ pages.

9. The index begins on page _____.

Name _____   Date _____

THE INDEX OF A BOOK

An *INDEX* is an alphabetical list of names, places, or topics found in a book or a catalog giving the page or place each can be found.

INDEX			
Apples	31, 33	Mars	60, 61
Atlantic Ocean	34-36	Mosquito	10
Chipmunk	4, 5-7	Mount Everest	46, 50-52, 54
Diamonds	25-28	Nylon	85
Elephants	6	Robins	2
Hawaii	42	Roses	9, 12
Indian Ocean	36-38, 40	Sahara Desert	75-77, 79
Lake Michigan	90	Sharks	63, 70-72

DIRECTIONS:

Fill in the answer on the blank line.

1. How many pages contain information on *Diamonds?* _____

2. How many pages contain information on *Mount Everest?* _____

3. Information on *Robins* will be found on page or pages _____.

4. Which would be the best information source for information on the *Indian Ocean?* _____.

5. Information on *Sharks* will be found on page or pages _____.

6. Information on the *Sahara Desert* will be found on page or pages _____ .

7. On what page or pages will you find information on the *Atlantic Ocean?* _____

8. How many pages will give you information on *Mars?* _____ .

9. You will find information on *Apples* on page or pages _____ .

10. Will you find two or four pages of information on *Roses?* _____ .

11. The _____ tells you that the pages between the numbers are included in the information.

12. The _____ tells you the pages between the numbers are not included in the information.

DECEMBER

Lesson 1

SKILL: Knowledge and understanding of alphabetizing.

OBJECTIVE: Students will practice the letters before and after a given letter.

LITERATURE: Fantasy and/or seasonal fiction and nonfiction.

PREPARATION: Print each letter of the alphabet on a separate 6 × 9-inch index card. Shuffle cards. Prepare introduction to fantasy and/or seasonal fiction and nonfiction. Display fantasy and/or seasonal fiction and nonfiction. Place folders on tables.

LESSON: Students take assigned seats. Check attendance. Hand out all letter cards. Call a letter. The person holding letter will come forward. Ask for the letter before that letter, then the letter after. Return to seat. Continue, calling for a letter and varying letters before and after until all variations have been called. Introduce genre. Tell briefly of books on display.

BOOK SELECTION: Students return to tables. Review lesson. Dismiss by tables. Collect folders.

Lesson 2

SKILL: Knowledge and understanding of alphabetizing.

OBJECTIVE: Students will practice alphabetizing to the second letter.

LITERATURE: Fantasy and/or seasonal fiction and nonfiction.

PREPARATION: Write the names of several authors on separate 3 × 5 cards. Ask students to alphabetize the names to the second letter. Prepare 8 to 10 per table group. Shuffle, band together. Display fantasy and/or seasonal fiction and nonfiction. Place folders on tables.

LESSON: Students take assigned seats. Check attendance. Give each table a set of cards. Have students alphabetize cards. Check, then exchange with another table. If time allows, interfile sets. Tell briefly of books on display.

BOOK SELECTION: Students return to tables. Review lesson. Dismiss by tables. Collect folders.

Lesson 3

SKILL: Knowledge and understanding of alphabetizing.

OBJECTIVE: Students will practice alphabetizing to the letter necessary.

LITERATURE: Fantasy and/or seasonal fiction and nonfiction.

PREPARATION: Write several subject headings on separate 3 × 5 cards. Ask students to alphabetize to any letter. Prepare 8 to 10 per table group. Shuffle, band together. Display fantasy and/or seasonal fiction and nonfiction. Place folders on tables.

LESSON: Students take assigned seats. Check attendance. Give each table a set of cards. Have students alphabetize cards. Check, exchange sets. If there is time, interfile sets. Tell briefly of books on display.

BOOK SELECTION: Students return to tables. Review lesson. Dismiss by tables. Collect folders.

Lesson 4

SKILL: Knowledge and understanding of alphabetizing.

OBJECTIVE: Students will practice alphabetizing authors, titles, and subjects.

LITERATURE: Fantasy and/or seasonal fiction and nonfiction.

PREPARATION: Write the titles of several books on separate 3 × 5 cards. Prepare 8 to 10 per table group. Shuffle, band together. Display fantasy and/or seasonal fiction and nonfiction. Place folders on tables.

LESSON: Students take assigned seats. Check attendance. Give each table a set of cards. Have students alphabetize cards. Check, exchange sets. If time allows, interfile author, title, and subject cards. Tell briefly of books on display.

BOOK SELECTION: Students return to tables. Review lesson. Dismiss by tables. Collect folders.

JANUARY

Lesson 1

SKILL: Knowledge and understanding of the card catalog.

OBJECTIVE: Students will be introduced to the card catalog. Students will be introduced to the author, title, and subject card.

LITERATURE: Animal fiction and nonfiction.

PREPARATION: Materials for introduction of card catalog. Make a photocopy of a set of catalog cards. Make a transparency from photocopy. Overhead projector. Prepare an introduction to animal fiction and nonfiction. Place folders on tables.

LESSON: Students take assigned seats. Check attendance. Introduce the card catalog. Using transparency, introduce and discuss the author, title, and subject card. Introduce animal fiction and nonfiction. Tell briefly of books on display.

BOOK SELECTION: Students return to tables. Review lesson. Dismiss by tables. Collect folders.

Lesson 2

SKILL: Knowledge and understanding of the outside guides of the card catalog.

OBJECTIVE: Students will practice using the outside guides of the card catalog.

LITERATURE: Animal fiction and nonfiction.

PREPARATION: On 8½ × 11 paper, prepare a master copy of the outside guides of your card catalog. (This may take time, but can be used over and over.) Make a copy for each student. Make a transparency for introduction. Overhead projector. A list of authors' names. Display animal fiction and nonfiction. Display animal fiction and nonfiction. Place folders on tables.

LESSON: Students take assigned seats. Check attendance. Using transparency, introduce outside guides. Practice locating proper drawer using students' names, then list of authors. Tell briefly of books on display.

BOOK SELECTION: Students return to tables. Review lesson. Dismiss by tables. Collect folders.

Lesson 3

SKILL: Knowledge and understanding of the outside guides of the card catalog.

OBJECTIVE: Students will practice using the outside guides of the card catalog.

LITERATURE: Animal fiction and nonfiction.

PREPARATION: Transparency of outside guides. Overhead projector. Make a list of titles and subjects found in your collection. Display animal fiction and nonfiction. Place folders on tables.

LESSON: Students take assigned seats. Check attendance. Using transparency, review locating proper drawer for authors. Using list, practice locating drawer for titles and subject. Tell briefly of books on display.

BOOK SELECTION: Students return to tables. Review lesson. Dismiss by tables. Collect folders.

Lesson 4

SKILL: Knowledge and understanding of the card catalog.

OBJECTIVE: Students will practice locating books on the shelf using the card catalog.

LITERATURE: Animal fiction and nonfiction.

PREPARATION: A copy of the activity "Locating Books on the Shelf" for each student. A transparency for introduction. Overhead projector. Place a catalog drawer for each two students on the tables. Place two activity sheets on each drawer. Display animal fiction and nonfiction. Place folders on tables.

LESSON: Students take assigned seats. Check attendance. Using transparency explain directions. Students work in pairs. Select a card, fill in the information. Using the sheet, locate the book on the shelf. Select another card and follow same procedure. Continue for length of period. Tell briefly of books on display.

BOOK SELECTION: Students return to tables. Review lesson. Dismiss by tables. Collect folders.

Name _____ Date _____

LOCATING BOOKS ON THE SHELF

Call Number	Kind of Card	Author	Title	Book Located

FEBRUARY

Lesson 1

SKILL: Practice with biography.

OBJECTIVE: Students will review biography and practice locating biography books on the shelf.

LITERATURE: Biography.

PREPARATION: A blank transparency. Overhead projector. Prepare an introduction to biography. Display biography. Place folders on tables.

LESSON: Students take assigned seats. Check attendance. Using transparency, review biography and how biography is shelved. Introduce biography project:

    1. Each person will select one biography that can be read in a week.

    2. Students will be given time to read in the classroom. (Arrange beforehand with classroom teacher.)

    3. Students will bring biography to class next week.

    4. Students will fill in an outline, then write a report on the biography, using a hornbook motif.

    Introduce biography collection.

BOOK SELECTION: Students return to tables. Review project. Dismiss by tables. Collect folders.

Lesson 2

SKILL: Knowledge and understanding of biography. Knowledge of hornbooks.

OBJECTIVE: Students will be introduced to hornbooks. Students will begin biography report.

LITERATURE: Biography.

PREPARATION: A copy of "Outline for Biography Hornbooks" for each student. A transparency for introduction. Overhead projector. Illustrations of hornbooks. Prepare a short talk on hornbooks. Display biography. Place folders on tables.

LESSON: Students take assigned seats. Check attendance. Students must have biography book. Introduce hornbooks. Introduce activity. Students complete activity. Tell briefly of books on display.

> *BOOK SELECTION:* Students return to tables. Review lesson. Dismiss by tables. Collect folders.

Lesson 3

SKILL: Preparing a short biographical report.

OBJECTIVE: Students will write a biographical report.

LITERATURE: Biography.

PREPARATION: A copy of the activity "Biography Hornbooks" for each student. A transparency for introduction. Overhead projector. Display biography. Place folders on tables. The hornbooks make an interesting bulletin board. Have materials ready if you plan a bulletin board.

> *LESSON:* Students take assigned seats. Check attendance. Using transparency, introduce activity. Have students complete activity or let them complete next week if extra time is needed. Tell briefly of books on display.
>
> *BOOK SELECTION:* Students return to tables. Review lesson. Dismiss by tables. Collect folders.

Lesson 4

SKILL: Knowledge and understanding of autobiography and collective biography.

OBJECTIVE: Students will review autobiography and collective biography.

LITERATURE: Biography.

PREPARATION: Display biography, autobiography, and collective biography. Place folders on tables.

> *LESSON:* Students take assigned seats. Check attendance. Complete biography report. Review autobiography and collective biography. Tell briefly of books on display.
>
> *BOOK SELECTION:* Students return to tables. Review lesson. Dismiss by tables. Collect folders.

Name _____   Date _____

OUTLINE FOR BIOGRAPHY HORNBOOK

A. Name of person

_____

B. Early life
   1. Birth date _____
   2. Place of birth _____
   3. Education _____

   _____

   _____

   _____

C. Contributions

   _____

   _____

   _____

   _____

   _____

   _____

D. Interesting facts

   _____

   _____

   _____

E. Death date _____

Name _____   Date _____

BIOGRAPHY HORNBOOK

MARCH

Lesson 1

SKILL: Knowledge and understanding of the encyclopedia.

OBJECTIVE: Students will be introduced to the encyclopedia and will practice locating the proper volume.

LITERATURE: Adventure fiction and nonfiction.

PREPARATION: Materials to introduce the encyclopedia included in your collection. Make a drawing of the spines of the encyclopedia or encyclopedias included in your collection. Make a transparency for introduction. Make a copy for each student. A copy of the activity "Selecting the Right Volume" for each student. Over Prepare an introduction to adventure fiction and nonfiction. Display genre. Place folders on tables.

LESSON: Students take assigned seats. Check attendance. Introduce encyclopedias. Introduce activity. Hand out activity. Have students complete activity. Collect to correct or correct together using transparency. Introduce adventure fiction and nonfiction. Tell briefly of books on display.

BOOK SELECTION: Students return to tables. Review lesson. Dismiss by tables. Collect folders.

Lesson 2

SKILL: Knowledge and understanding of the encyclopedia.

OBJECTIVE: Students will practice using guide words.

LITERATURE: Adventure fiction and nonfiction.

PREPARATION: A copy of the activity "Guide Words" for each student. A transparency for introduction. Overhead projector. Display genre. Place folders on tables.

LESSON: Students take assigned seats. Check attendance. Introduce activity. Have students complete activity. Collect to correct or correct together using transparency. Tell briefly of books on display.

BOOK SELECTION: Students return to tables. Review lesson. Dismiss by tables. Collect folders.

Lesson 3

SKILL: Knowledge and understanding of the encyclopedia.

OBJECTIVE: Students will practice determining the key word.

LITERATURE: Adventure fiction and nonfiction.

PREPARATION: A copy of the activity "Using Key Words" for each student. A transparency for introduction. Overhead projector. Display adventure fiction and nonfiction. Place folders on tables.

LESSON: Students take assigned seats. Check attendance. Review previous lessons. Introduce key words, using transparency. Hand out activity. Have students complete activity. Collect to correct. Complete activity with class on transparency. Tell briefly of books on display.

BOOK SELECTION: Students return to tables. Review lesson. Dismiss by tables. Collect folders.

Lesson 4

SKILL: Knowledge and understanding of the encyclopedia.

OBJECTIVE: Students will practice locating information in the encyclopedia.

LITERATURE: Adventure fiction and nonfiction.

PREPARATION: Activity from last week. Transparency of activity. Overhead projector. Display adventure fiction and nonfiction. Place folders on tables.

LESSON: Students take assigned seats. Check attendance. Pass back activity. Introduce activity, using transparency. Have students locate information in encyclopedia. Using transparency, correct activity with class. Tell briefly of books on display.

BOOK SELECTION: Students return to tables. Review lesson. Dismiss by tables. Collect folders.

Name _____   Date _____

SELECTING THE RIGHT VOLUME

ENCYCLOPEDIA TITLE _____

DIRECTIONS: In what volume of the encyclopedia will the following subjects be found? Write the letters and number of the volume on the line following the subject.

1. MAURICE SENDAK _____
2. JANUARY _____
3. MOTORCYCLES _____
4. PACIFIC OCEAN _____
5. CATS _____
6. WATER POLO _____
7. COMPUTER _____
8. WINSLOW HOMER _____
9. FLAG DAY _____
10. SATURDAY _____

11. HORSES _____
12. FORT NIAGARA _____
13. DOMINION DAY _____
14. MESA VERDE _____
15. GLACIER BAY _____
16. DETROIT _____
17. VOODOOISM _____
18. LAURA INGALLS WILDER _____
19. FOOTBALL _____
20. QUEBEC CITY _____

Name _____   Date _____

GUIDE WORDS

Guide words are aids that help you find the key word. In encyclopedias, they are located at the upper left and right of the pages. The guide word or words at the left is the first entry on the page while the guide word or words at the right is the last entry on the page.

If the key word you are locating is alphabetized after the guide word at the left, but before the guide word on the right, the key word is on that page.

DIRECTIONS: Using the guide words below, check the key words in each exercise that would be found on those pages.

1. | Asia   Austria |

Ash _____   Australia _____
Arrow _____   Autograph _____
Aspen _____   Award _____
Atlas _____   Aviation _____

Mold _____   Meat _____
Money _____   Milk _____
Mica _____   Molasses _____
Mexico _____   Monday _____

2. | Mercury   Mole |

Pilgrims _____   Piano _____
Pistol _____   Phonograph _____
Pencil _____   Pavement _____
Pine _____   Pony Express _____

3. | Paste   Pigeon |

Truck _____   Throat _____
Tortilla _____   Television _____
Thistle _____   Triangle _____
Town _____   Tiger _____

4. | Theater   Tree |

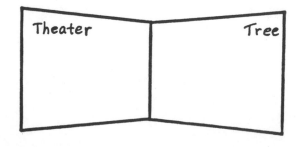

Name _____   Date _____

USING KEY WORDS

DIRECTIONS: 1. Underline the *key word* in each sentence.
2. Using the key word, locate the answer to each question in the encyclopedia.

EXAMPLE: What is the name of the longest *river* in the world?
(Answer: Nile River).

1. What was John Chapman's nickname?

   Answer: _____

2. What is the birthstone for September?

   Answer: _____

3. In what state is Russell Cave located?

   Answer: _____

4. What is the nickname for Ursa Minor?

   Answer: _____

5. In what state is the Mojave Desert located?

   Answer: _____

6. What is the name of the highest mountain in the world?

   Answer: _____

7. How many eyes do grasshoppers have?

   Answer: _____

8. In what country is the city of Cairo located?

   Answer: _____

9. In what year was Abraham Lincoln born?

   Answer: _____

APRIL

Lesson 1

SKILL: Knowledge and understanding of the atlas.

OBJECTIVE: Students will be introduced to the atlas.

LITERATURE: Science fiction.

PREPARATION: An atlas for every two students. A filmstrip or other media to introduce the atlas. Prepare an introduction to science fiction. Display science fiction. Place folders on tables.

LESSON: Students take assigned seats. Check attendance. Introduce and discuss maps, different types of maps, and the uses of maps. Introduce and discuss physical and political maps. Have students locate one of each in atlas. Introduce and discuss longitude and latitude. Show filmstrip or use other media. Introduce science fiction. Tell briefly of books on display.

BOOK SELECTION: Students return to tables. Review lesson. Dismiss by tables. Collect folders.

Lesson 2

SKILL: Knowledge and understanding of the atlas.

OBJECTIVE: Students will locate places in the atlas using the key.

LITERATURE: Science fiction.

PREPARATION: A copy of the same map for every two students. A transparency of map for introduction. Overhead projector. A 12- to 15-inch length of string for each student. Display science fiction. Place folders on tables.

LESSON: Students take assigned seats. Check attendance. Review maps. Hand out materials. Students work together in twos. Assign one to be A — latitude — and the other B — longitude. Pick a place on the map. Give key. A places string down, B places string across. Answer will be where string intersects. Repeat process. Tell briefly of books on display.

BOOK SELECTION: Students return to tables. Review lesson. Dismiss by tables. Collect folders.

Lesson 3

SKILL: Knowledge and understanding of the atlas.

OBJECTIVE: Students will locate places in the atlas using the key.

LITERATURE: Science fiction.

PREPARATION: The maps and string, and transparency from last week's lesson. Overhead projector. A sheet of paper for each two students. Display science fiction. Place folders on tables.

LESSON: Students take assigned seats. Check attendance. Review the use of maps. Hand out map, string, and paper. Each group will study the map and locate several places of their choice. They will write down the place and key. In turn, each group will ask class to locate place through giving place and key. Location will then be shown on the transparency. Continue until all have had a turn. Tell briefly of books on display.

BOOK SELECTION: Students return to tables. Review lesson. Dismiss by tables. Collect folders.

Lesson 4

SKILL: Knowledge and understanding of the atlas.

OBJECTIVE: Students will demonstrate their ability to use the atlas through completion of an activity sheet.

LITERATURE: Science fiction.

PREPARATION: An atlas for every two students. A copy of the activity "Atlas Practice" for each student. A transparency for introduction. Overhead projector. Display science fiction. Place folders on tables.

LESSON: Students take assigned seats. Check attendance. Hand out materials. Using transparency, introduce activity. Have students complete activity. Collect to correct. Complete activity on transparency with class. Tell briefly of books on display.

BOOK SELECTION: Students return to tables. Review lesson. Dismiss by tables. Collect folders.

Name _____   Date _____

ATLAS PRACTICE

DIRECTIONS: 1. Underline the key word.
2. Using an atlas, locate the answers.

1. What two states form a border with Florida?

   Answer: _____

2. In what country is James Bay located?

   Answer: _____

3. In what state is the Great Salt Lake located?

   Answer: _____

4. In what state is the city of Denver located?

   Answer: _____

5. What states form a border with the state of Oregon?

   Answer: _____

6. What states form a border with the country of Mexico?

   Answer: _____

7. In what province is the city of Toronto located?

   Answer: _____

8. On what lake is the city of Chicago located?

   Answer: _____

MAY

Lesson 1

SKILL: Practice in the use of the encyclopedia and the atlas.

OBJECTIVE: Students will begin a project designed to afford practice in the use of the encyclopedia and the atlas.

LITERATURE: Fables.

PREPARATION: This project involves the cooperation of the classroom teacher. The completed project will be displayed in the classroom. Make an outline of the United States. Using transparency, draw a map on the classroom bulletin board. A copy of the activity "United States Project" for each student. A copy of the state slips, cut up. Construction paper, tracing paper, and crayons. Prepare an introduction to fables. Display fables. Place folders on tables.

LESSON: Students take assigned seats. Check attendance. Introduce project. Each student will select a state and begin locating the information requested on activity sheet. Students will trace the state during the week in the classroom, and bring to class next week. Introduce fables. Tell briefly of books on display.

BOOK SELECTION: Students return to tables. Review project. Dismiss by tables. Collect folders.

Lesson 2

SKILL: Practice in the use of the encyclopedia and the atlas.

OBJECTIVE: Students will continue the project.

LITERATURE: Fables.

PREPARATION: Materials for the project. Display fables. Place folders on tables.

LESSON: Students take assigned seats. Check attendance. Have students continue project. Tell briefly of books on display.

BOOK SELECTION: Students return to tables. Review progress of project. Dismiss by tables. Collect folders.

Lesson 3

SKILL: Practice in the use of the encyclopedia and atlas.

OBJECTIVE: Students will continue project.

LITERATURE: Fables.

PREPARATION: Materials for project. Display fables. Place folders on tables.

LESSON: Students take assigned seats. Check attendance. Have students continue project. Some students may have time to select another state or remaining states could be covered by students working together. All states must be completed. Tell briefly of books on display.

BOOK SELECTION: Students return to tables. Review progress of project. Project is to be completed next week. Dismiss by tables. Collect folders.

Lesson 4

SKILL: Practice in the use of the encyclopedia and atlas.

OBJECTIVE: Students will complete the project.

LITERATURE: Fables.

PREPARATION: Materials to complete project. Display fables. Place folders on tables.

LESSON: Students take assigned seats. Check attendance. Continue and complete project. Tell briefly of books on display.

BOOK SELECTION: Students return to tables. Review and discuss the results of the project. Dismiss by tables. Collect folders. Visit the classroom to view the results of the project.

STATE SLIPS

DIRECTIONS: Cut out the slips and put them into a box. Have each student select one to determine the state that will be researched. Students who complete the project may select another. Try to have all states represented to make a completed map.

ALABAMA	ALASKA	ARIZONA	ARKANSAS	CALIFORNIA
COLORADO	CONNECTICUT	DELAWARE	FLORIDA	GEORGIA
HAWAII	IDAHO	ILLINOIS	INDIANA	IOWA
KANSAS	KENTUCKY	LOUISIANA	MAINE	MARYLAND
MASSACHUSETTS	MICHIGAN	MINNESOTA	MISSISSIPPI	MISSOURI
MONTANA	NEBRASKA	NEVADA	NEW HAMPSHIRE	NEW JERSEY
NEW MEXICO	NEW YORK	NORTH CAROLINA	NORTH DAKOTA	OHIO
OKLAHOMA	OREGON	PENNSYLVANIA	RHODE ISLAND	SOUTH CAROLINA
SOUTH DAKOTA	TENNESSEE	TEXAS	UTAH	VERMONT
VIRGINIA	WASHINGTON	WEST VIRGINIA	WISCONSIN	WYOMING

Name _____   Date _____

UNITED STATES PROJECT

DIRECTIONS

1. Select a slip bearing the name of a state.

   Name of state _____

2. Locate the following information:

   Capital _____   State bird _____

   Population _____   State flower _____

   Date of statehood _____   State tree _____

3. Trace your state using the map in the classroom.

4. Locate and label the capital.

5. Transfer the tracing to colored construction paper.

6. Cut out the outline of the state.

7. Label the information from #2 onto the paper. If the state is too small to label the information on the state, label the information on a square of the same colored construction paper and put near the state.

8. Paste state into place on large map. Outline with black marker.

9. Select another state if time and number of students allow.

JUNE

Lesson 1

SKILL: Review and reinforcement of the card catalog.

OBJECTIVE: Students will complete an activity designed to afford review of the card catalog.

LITERATURE: Humorous fiction and nonfiction.

PREPARATION: A copy of activity "Card Catalog Puzzle" for each student. Transparency for introduction. Prepare an introduction to humorous fiction and nonfiction. Display humorous fiction and nonfiction. Place folders on tables.

LESSON: Students take assigned seats. Check attendance. Hand out activity. Using transparency, introduce activity. Have students complete the activity. Complete the activity together on transparency. Introduce humorous fiction and nonfiction. Tell briefly of books on display.

BOOK SELECTION: Students return to tables. Review areas of the card catalog that students need. Dismiss by tables. Collect folders.

Lesson 2

SKILL: Review and reinforcement of library terms and concepts.

OBJECTIVE: Students will complete an activity designed to afford review and reinforcement of library terms and concepts.

LITERATURE: Humorous fiction and nonfiction.

PREPARATION: A copy of activity "Book Terms Scramble" for each student. A transparency for introduction. Overhead projector. Display humorous fiction and nonfiction. Place folders on tables.

LESSON: Students take assigned seats. Check attendance. Hand out activity. Using transparency, introduce activity. Have students complete activity. Complete activity together on transparency. Tell briefly of books on display.

BOOK SELECTION: Students return to tables. Review lesson. Dismiss by tables. Collect folders.

Lesson 3

SKILL: Review and reinforcement of the encyclopedia and the atlas.

OBJECTIVE: Students will complete an activity designed to reinforce the use of the encyclopedia and atlas.

LITERATURE: Humorous fiction and nonfiction.

PREPARATION: A copy of the activity "A Bouquet of Facts" for each student. A transparency for introduction. Overhead projector. Atlases and encyclopedias. Display humorous fiction and nonfiction. Place folders on tables.

LESSON: Students take assigned seats. Check attendance. Hand out activity. Students complete activity. Complete activity with class on transparency. Tell briefly of books on display.

BOOK SELECTION: Students return to tables. Review lesson. Dismiss by tables. Collect folders.

Lesson 4

SKILL: Review of authors and book characters.

OBJECTIVE: Students will review and reinforce their knowledge of authors and book characters through a designed activity.

LITERATURE: As this is the last lesson of the year, there will be no book selection.

PREPARATION: A copy of the activity "Authors and Characters" for each student. A transparency for introduction. Overhead projector. Place folders on tables.

LESSON: Students take assigned seats. Check attendance. Hand out activity. Introduce activity using transparency. Have students complete activity. Complete together with class, using transparency. Folders go home with students. Discuss any summer reading programs available in the area. Dismiss by tables.

Name _____   Date _____

CARD CATALOG PUZZLE

ACROSS

3. If the call number contains numbers and letters, the book is _____ _____.

6. There are _____ main kinds of catalog cards.

7. The last line on a catalog card tells the number of _____.

11. The title is on the top line on a _____ card.

12. The card catalog is filed in _____ order.

13. The symbol © stands for _____ _____.

14. The author's name is on the top line on an _____ card.

DOWN

1. The card catalog is the _____ to the library's collection.

2. 921, 92, and B are the call numbers for _____.

4. Catalog cards are filed in _____ _____.

5. The company that produces the book is called the _____.

8. The _____ is located in the upper left hand corner of a catalog card.

9. The top line of a _____ card is in capital letters.

10. If the call number contains only letters, the book is _____.

Name _____   Date _____

BOOK TERMS SCRAMBLE

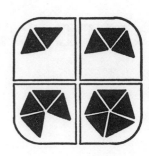

DIRECTIONS: The answers to the following questions are all mixed up. Can you unscramble them?

1. The person who wrote the book.
   HUTARO
   _____

2. The person who drew the pictures.
   ROARTULILST
   _____

3. The pictures themselves.
   ISNARTOLULIST
   _____

4. The name of the book.
   ITTLE
   _____

5. The company that produces the book.
   BLUSHIPER
   _____

6. Where the company is located.
   CALPE FO PLAINIBOUCT
   _____

7. The right to copy.
   THIRPCOGY
   _____

8. The date the book is published.
   PROTHCIGY TADE
   _____

9. The backbone of the book.
   SNIPE
   _____

10. Who ever is most important in a story.
    AMIN TRARACHEC
    _____

11. Where the story takes place.
    TENIGST
    _____

12. What the story is all about.
    POLT
    _____

13. The three sections or parts of a story.
    GENINGIBN
    _____

    DELDIM
    _____

    DEN
    _____

Name _____   Date _____

A BOUQUET OF FACTS

1. In what country is the Eiffel Tower located? _____

2. Find the name of a river in Brazil. _____

3. Find the name of a country in Europe. _____

4. What is the population of London? _____

5. What provinces border the province of Alberta? _____

6. What is the state flower of Massachusetts? _____

7. What sea separates England from mainland Europe? _____

8. What is the state tree of Rhode Island? _____

9. In what country is the city of Dublin located? _____

10. What country in South America is very long and very narrow? _____

Can you pick a full bouquet?

Use the encyclopedia or atlas to find the answers. If you find them all, you have a full bouquet.

AUTHORS AND CHARACTERS

DIRECTIONS: Find the authors and characters listed below in the word search. They may be found forwards, backwards, up, down, or diagonally.

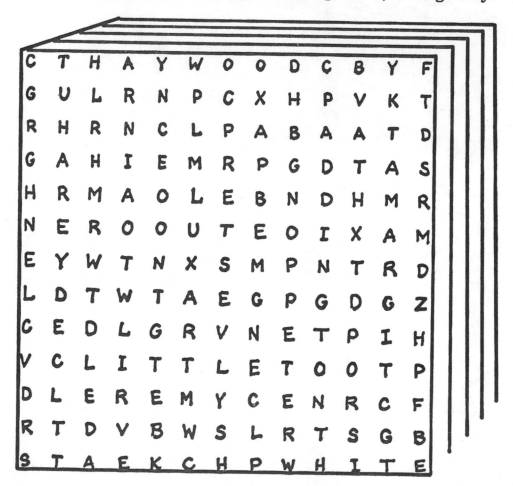

```
C T H A Y W O O D C B Y F
G U L R N P C X H P V K T
R H R N C L P A B A A T D
G A H I E M R P G D T A S
H R M A O L E B N D H M R
N E R O O U T E O I X A M
E Y W T N X S M P N T R D
L D T W T A E G P G D G Z
C E D L G R V N E T P I H
V C L I T T L E T O O T P
D L E R E M Y C E N R C F
R T D V B W S L R T S G B
S T A E K C H P W H I T E
```

Now match the author on the left with the character he or she created. Draw a line from the author to the character.

authors	*characters*
BOND	CHARLOTTE
CLEARY	CURIOUS GEORGE
GRAMATKY	EDDIE
HAYWOOD	HARRY
KEATS	LITTLE TOOT
H. A. REY	MAX
SENDAK	PADDINGTON
STEIG	PETER
WHITE	RAMONA
ZION	SYLVESTER

GRADE 4

OVERVIEW

The main objectives in fourth grade are:
- to correlate the skills closely with the classroom academic curriculum.
- to continue to introduce and reinforce parts of the book and parts of the story.
- to reinforce the use of periodicals as reference tools.
- to introduce, review, and reinforce card catalog skills.
- to introduce and reinforce individual reference tools: author books, biographical dictionaries, gazeteers, atlases, and almanacs.
- to introduce the proper form of a bibliography.
- to continue to review and reinforce encyclopedia skills.
- to review and reinforce the Dewey Decimal Classification System.
- to continue to introduce different genres to continue to develop students' interest areas.

Terms, Concepts, and Skills To Be Introduced or Reinforced

Parts of the Book
  Glossary
  Frontispiece
  Preface, foreword, or introduction
  Verso page
Parts of the Story
  Dialogue
  Action
Anthologies
Author reference tools
Biographical dictionaries
Gazeteers or geographical dictionaries
Card Catalog Skills
  Catalog cards: author, title, subject
  Decoding information on a catalog card
  Cross references
  Location of materials on shelf

Dewey Decimal Classification System
  Ten main classes
Bibliography
Encyclopedias
  Locating volume
  Cross-references
  Headings
  Paraphrasing
Periodicals

Literature: Monthly Genre

Family-School   Fantasy
Mystery-Detective   Biography
Historical   Science Fiction
Seasonal   Humorous
Animal   Foreign Setting

SEPTEMBER

Lesson 1

SKILL: Knowledge of library procedures. Knowledge of the various sections of the library.

OBJECTIVE: Students will review and reinforce their knowledge of the procedures of the library and the library's resources.

LITERATURE: Family and school fiction and nonfiction.

PREPARATION: A copy of "Orientation Skills." Paste onto tagboard and laminate. Cut into cards. Prepare an introduction to family and school fiction and nonfiction. Display family and school fiction and nonfiction. Class roster.

LESSON: Students sit where they wish. Permanent seating will be assigned next week. Check attendance. Students will begin recording books read next week. Give each table a card. Each group or table is to locate the answers to the questions on the card. Each group will report questions and answers to the class. Discuss as necessary. Introduce family and school fiction and nonfiction. Tell briefly of books on display.

BOOK SELECTION: Students return to tables. Review lesson. Dismiss by tables.

Lesson 2

SKILL: Record keeping of books read and designing folders.

OBJECTIVE: Students will design an appropriate folder and will begin to record books read during the week.

LITERATURE: Family and school fiction and nonfiction.

PREPARATION: A 12 × 16 piece of construction paper of tagboard for each student. Crayons. A copy of the "Reading Record" for each student. Plan permanent seating arrangement. A 4 × 6 sheet of paper for table number. Display family and school fiction and nonfiction.

LESSON: Students take assigned seats. Check attendance. Students record books read during the week. Students will fold paper to make a folder and decorate folders. Tell briefly of books on display.

BOOK SELECTION: Students return to tables. Folders are to be put in middle of table with table number on top. Review lesson. Dismiss by tables. Collect folders.

Lesson 3

SKILL: Knowledge and understanding of the parts of the story: dialogue and action.

OBJECTIVE: Students will review the parts of the story: characters, setting, and plot. Students will be introduced to dialogue and action.

LITERATURE: Family and school fiction and nonfiction.

PREPARATION: A blank transparency. Overhead projector. Display family and school fiction and nonfiction. Place folders on tables.

LESSON: Students take assigned seats. Check attendance while students record books read during the week. Using transparency, review and discuss the parts of the story. Introduce and discuss dialogue and action. Tell briefly of books on display.

BOOK SELECTION: Students return to tables. Review lesson. Dismiss by tables. Collect folders.

Lesson 4

SKILL: Knowledge and understanding of the parts of the book.

OBJECTIVE: Students will review title page, tables of contents, and index. Students will be introduced to the glossary.

LITERATURE: Family and school fiction and nonfiction.

PREPARATION: A blank transparency. Overhead projector. Several books having a glossary on each table. Display family and school fiction and nonfiction. Place folders on tables.

LESSON: Students take assigned seats. Check attendance while students record books read during the week. Using transparency, list and discuss the title page, table of contents, and index. Introduce the glossary. Have students find and use glossary in books on tables. Tell briefly of books on display.

BOOK SELECTION: Students return to tables. Review lesson. Dismiss by tables. Collect folders.

ORIENTATION SKILLS

1. FICTION

DEMONSTRATE TO THE CLASS:

1. where the fiction section begins and ends.
2. how fiction is arranged.
3. the call number for fiction.
4. where a book by the following authors would be found:
   Beverly Cleary
   Carolyn Haywood
   Laura Ingalls Wilder
5. different types of fiction books.

2. NON-FICTION

DEMONSTRATE TO THE CLASS:

1. where the nonfiction section begins and ends.
2. how nonfiction is arranged?
3. where the subject, Fairy Tales, 398 and 398.2 would be located.
4. where the subject, Birds, 598.2 would be located.
5. where the subject, Sports, 796s would be located.
6. where the subject, History of the U.S., 973s, would be located.
7. meaning of nonfiction.

3. BIOGRAPHY

DEMONSTRATE TO THE CLASS:

1. where the biography section begins and ends.
2. the meaning of biography.
3. the call number for Biography.
4. the call number for collective Biography.
5. where a book about Abraham Lincoln would be located.
6. where a book about George Washington would be located.
7. reasons for reading biography.

4. PICTURE BOOK SECTION

DEMONSTRATE TO THE CLASS:

1. the beginning and end of the picture book section.
2. the beginning and end of the 'I Can Read' section.
3. the difference between picture books and 'I Can Read' books.
4. the call number for picture books and 'I Can Read' books.
5. how picture books and 'I Can Read' books are arranged.
6. where a book by C.W. Anderson would be located.
7. where a book by H.A. Rey would be located.

ORIENTATION SKILLS
(continued)

5. REFERENCE COLLECTION

DEMONSTRATE TO THE CLASS:

1. where encyclopedias are located.
2. where atlases are located.
3. where almanacs are located.
4. where dictionaries are located.
5. where other reference materials in the collection are located.
6. the circulation rules for reference books.
7. the mark on the spine that denotes a reference book.

6. MAGAZINE SECTION

DEMONSTRATE TO THE CLASS:

1. where magazine section is located.
2. circulation rules for magazines.
3. tell briefly about magazines available, titles and contents.

7. PLACES AND BEHAVIOR

DEMONSTRATE AND GIVE INFORMATION REGARDING:

1. location and purpose of circulation desk.
2. location of returning books area.
3. location and use of workroom.
4. rules of behavior in the library.

8. CIRCULATION RULES

DEMONSTRATE AND GIVE INFORMATION REGARDING:

1. sign-out procedures
2. rules such as
   a. How many books may be borrowed at one time.
   b. For how long a period the books may be borrowed.
   c. How to renew a book.
   d. How to reserve a book.
3. the overdue process and procedures.

_____ 's READING RECORD

AUTHOR   TITLE

OCTOBER

Lesson 1

SKILL: Knowledge and understanding of the Dewey Decimal Classification System.

OBJECTIVE: Students will review and add to their knowledge of the Dewey Decimal Classification System.

LITERATURE: Mystery and detective fiction and nonfiction.

PREPARATION: A copy of the sheet "Melvil Dewey" for each student. A transparency of the sheet. Overhead projector. Materials to introduce Dewey. Prepare an introduction to mystery and detective fiction and nonfiction. Display mystery and detective fiction. Place folders on tables.

LESSON: Students take assigned seats. Check attendance. Introduce and discuss Dewey. Emphasize the main classes. Introduce mystery and detective fiction and nonfiction. Tell briefly of books on display.

BOOK SELECTION: Students return to tables. Review lesson. Dismiss by tables. Collect folders.

Lesson 2

SKILL: Knowledge and understanding of the Dewey Decimal Classification System.

OBJECTIVE: Students will become familiar with subjects included in each main class.

LITERATURE: Mystery and detective fiction and nonfiction.

PREPARATION: A copy of activity sheet "Dewey's Journey" for each student. A transparency to introduce activity. Overhead projector. Display mystery and detective fiction and nonfiction. Place folders on tables.

LESSON: Students take assigned seats. Check attendance. Divide class into ten groups. Assign each group a main class. Each group will complete activity based on a class. Each group will report back to class. Tell briefly of books on display.

BOOK SELECTION: Students return to tables. Review lesson. Dismiss by tables. Collect folders.

Lesson 3

SKILL: Knowledge and understanding of the Dewey Decimal Classification System.

OBJECTIVE: Students will practice assigning Dewey main class numbers to subjects.

LITERATURE: Mystery and detective fiction and nonfiction.

PREPARATION: A copy of the activity "Practice With Dewey" for each student. A transparency for introduction. Overhead projector. Display mystery and detective fiction and nonfiction. Place folders on tables.

LESSON: Students take assigned seats. Check attendance. Review the ten main classes. Hand out activity sheets. Introduce activity, using the transparency. Have students complete activity. Collect to correct. Complete activity with class on transparency. Tell briefly of books on display.

BOOK SELECTION: Students return to tables. Review lesson. Ask students to choose a favorite subject for next week. Dismiss by tables. Collect folders.

Lesson 4

SKILL: Knowledge and understanding of the Dewey Decimal Classification System.

OBJECTIVE: Students will illustrate their favorite subject and label the subject with the proper Dewey number.

LITERATURE: Mystery and detective fiction and nonfiction.

PREPARATION: Construction or drawing paper and crayons for each student. Display mystery and detective fiction and nonfiction. Place folders on tables.

LESSON: Students take assigned seats. Check attendance. Have students choose favorite subject, illustrate that subject, and assign the Dewey number. Display around library. Tell briefly of books on display.

BOOK SELECTION: Students return to tables. Review lesson. Dismiss by tables. Collect folders.

MELVIL DEWEY

Melvil Dewey is remembered as the person most responsible for the sound development of library science.

TIME LINE

1851 Melvil Dewey was born at Adams Center, New York, December 10, 1851.

1874 Dewey graduated from Amherst College, Amherst, Massachusetts.

1874 Dewey became acting librarian at Amherst College.

1876 Dewey was one of the founders of the American Library Association which was established in 1876.

1877 Dewey moved to Boston where he founded and edited *Library Journal*.

1883 Dewey became librarian at Columbia College in New York City. He founded the School of Library Economy, the first school established to train librarians. This school was reestablished in Albany, New York as the State Library School and which is today part of the State University of New York system.

1889 Dewey became director of the New York State Library, a post that he held until 1906.

1889 Dewey became secretary of the University of New York.

1904 Dewey became New York State Director of Libraries.

1931 Dewey died on December 31, 1931.

While Melvil Dewey was working in the library at Amherst, he devised the classification system. At that time, libraries were organized according to the whim of the librarian. Dewey believed that if one system was used, patrons could retrieve materials from any library. The system he devised and proposed was designed so well that it is still widely used today.

THE TEN MAIN CLASSES OF THE DEWEY DECIMAL CLASSIFICATION SYSTEM

000–099	REFERENCE	500–599	SCIENCE
100–199	PHILOSOPHY & PSYCHOLOGY	600–699	APPLIED SCIENCE
		700–799	FINE ARTS
200–299	RELIGION	800–899	LITERATURE
300–399	SOCIAL SCIENCE	900–999	HISTORY, GEOGRAPHY, BIOGRAPHY
400–499	LANGUAGE		

Name _____   Date _____

DEWEY'S JOURNEY
STATION # _____

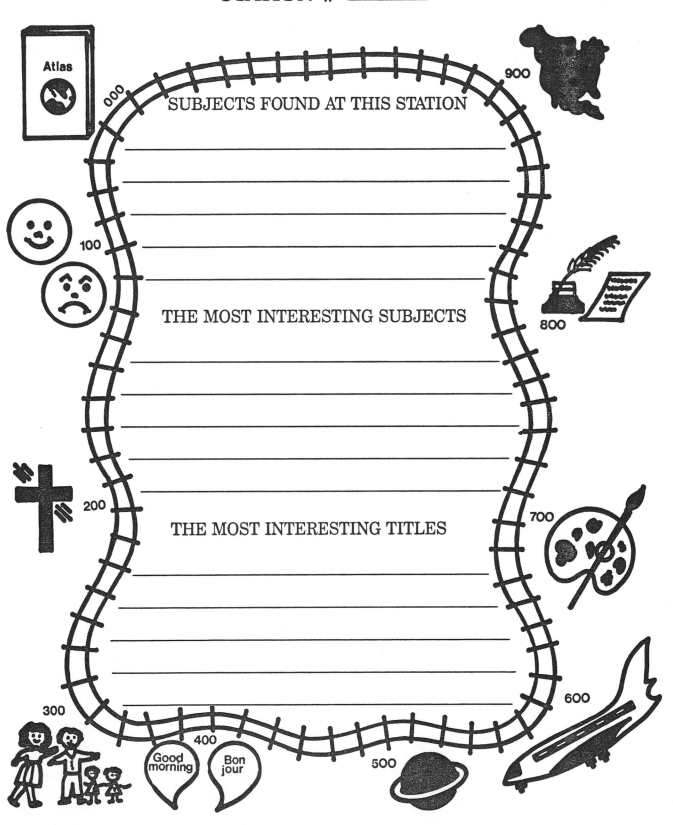

Atlas

SUBJECTS FOUND AT THIS STATION

_____
_____
_____
_____
_____

THE MOST INTERESTING SUBJECTS

_____
_____
_____
_____

THE MOST INTERESTING TITLES

_____
_____
_____
_____

000   100   200   300   400   500   600   700   800   900

Good morning   Bon jour

Name _____   Date _____

PRACTICE WITH DEWEY

DIRECTIONS: Assign the Dewey main class number to the subjects below.

1. AIRPLANES	_____	11. DANCE	_____
2. BIOGRAPHY	_____	12. COWBOYS	_____
3. TELEVISION	_____	13. MATHEMATICS	_____
4. HOLIDAYS	_____	14. WEATHER	_____
5. PHOTOGRAPHY	_____	15. ITALIAN LANGUAGE	_____
6. EMOTIONS	_____	16. POETRY	_____
7. TUNNELS	_____	17. MANNERS	_____
8. DESERTS	_____	18. SIGN LANGUAGE	_____
9. CANADA	_____	19. DREAMS	_____
10. ENCYCLOPEDIAS	_____	20. GREEK MYTHS	_____

NOVEMBER

Lesson 1

SKILL: Knowledge and understanding of magazines for curriculum and personal information.

OBJECTIVE: Students will become more familiar with the magazine titles available in the collection.

LITERATURE: Historical fiction and nonfiction.

PREPARATION: A transparency of titles available. Overhead projector. Copies of each title on tables. Prepare an introduction to historical fiction and nonfiction. Display historical fiction and nonfiction. Place folders on tables.

LESSON: Students take assigned seats. Check attendance. Using transparency, introduce the titles available. Students will carefully read through each title to become familiar with each title. They will choose or be assigned one title next week to research. Introduce historical fiction and nonfiction. Tell briefly of books on display.

BOOK SELECTION: Students return to tables. Review lesson. Dismiss by tables. Collect folders.

Lesson 2

SKILL: Knowledge and understanding of magazines for curriculum and personal information.

OBJECTIVE: Students will begin a project designed to provide deeper insight into the use of magazines.

LITERATURE: Historical fiction and nonfiction.

PREPARATION: A copy of the activity "BE A MAGAZINE EXPERT" for each title of magazine available. Divide class into as many groups as there are magazine titles. A transparency for introduction of activity. Overhead projector. Display historical fiction and nonfiction. Place folders on tables.

LESSON: Students take assigned seats. Check attendance. Introduce activity. Divide into groups. Assign titles. Hand out activity sheets. Groups will have two weeks to complete activity. Tell briefly of books on display.

BOOK SELECTION: Students return to tables. Review progress of activity. Dismiss by tables. Collect folders.

Lesson 3

SKILL: Knowledge and understanding of magazines for curriculum and personal enjoyment.

OBJECTIVE: Students will continue and complete magazine reports.

LITERATURE: Historical fiction and nonfiction.

PREPARATION: Transparency of activity. Overhead projector. Display historical fiction and nonfiction. Place folders on tables.

> *LESSON:* Students take assigned seats. Check attendance. Review activity. Students complete activity. Students will report to class next week on their title. Display historical fiction and nonfiction.
>
> *BOOK SELECTION:* Students return to tables. Review lesson. Dismiss by tables. Collect folders.

Lesson 4

SKILL: Knowledge and understanding of magazines for curriculum and personal information.

OBJECTIVE: Students will report to class on the title of magazine each group researched.

LITERATURE: Historical fiction and nonfiction.

PREPARATION: A sheet of paper for each student. Display historical fiction and nonfiction. Place folders on tables.

> *LESSON:* Students take assigned seats. Check attendance. Give groups a few minutes to go over reports. Have each group report to class on their title. Students will take notes and ask questions following each presentation. Tell briefly of books on display.
>
> *BOOK SELECTION:* Students return to tables. Review magazine unit. Dismiss by tables. Collect folders.

Group members _____

_____

_____

Date _____

BE A MAGAZINE EXPERT

DIRECTIONS: 1. Work as a group, sharing questions.
2. Become experts on the magazine.
3. Fill in the following information.

1. Title of magazine _____

2. How often is the magazine published? _____

3. What is the cost of a subscription? _____

4. Name of publisher _____

5. Name of editor _____

6. Check the contents of the magazine. Does it contain?

Fiction	Yes ___ No ___		Puzzles	Yes _____	No _____
Nonfiction	Yes ___ No ___		Jokes	Yes _____	No _____
Games	Yes ___ No ___		Cartoons	Yes _____	No _____
Handcrafts	Yes ___ No ___		Other	Yes _____	No _____

7. Does each issue of the magazine have a theme?
Yes _____ No _____

8. Would the magazine help with school assignments or is it mainly for leisure reading or both? Explain.

_____

9. For what grade level is the magazine most appropriate?

_____

10. Does the magazine have any material written by children?

_____

11. On the back of this sheet write your opinion of the magazine.

DECEMBER

Lesson 1

SKILL: Knowledge and understanding of the frontispiece of a book.

OBJECTIVE: Students will be introduced to the frontispiece and be able to locate the frontispiece in a book.

LITERATURE: Fantasy/Seasonal fiction and nonfiction.

PREPARATION: A blank transparency. Overhead projector. A piece of lined paper for each student. Place books containing a frontispiece on each table. Prepare an introduction to fantasy/seasonal fiction and nonfiction. Display fantasy/seasonal fiction and nonfiction. Place folders on tables.

LESSON: Students take assigned seats. Check attendance. Use transparency to review the parts of the book. Introduce frontispiece: a drawing or illustration opposite the title page. Have students locate the frontispiece in the books on tables. Write the term and definition on transparency. Have students copy onto paper. Introduce fantasy/seasonal fiction and nonfiction. Tell briefly of books on display.

BOOK SELECTION: Students return to tables. Students will check to see if their books contain a frontispiece. Show to class. Review lesson. Dismiss by tables. Collect folders.

Lesson 2

SKILL: Knowledge and understanding of the verso page.

OBJECTIVE: Students will be introduced to the verso page and be able to locate the verso page.

LITERATURE: Fantasy/seasonal fiction and nonfiction.

PREPARATION: A blank transparency. Overhead projector. Display fantasy/seasonal fiction and nonfiction. Place folders on tables.

LESSON: Students take assigned seats. Check attendance. Using transparency, review frontispiece. Introduce the verso page: the back of the title page and also the left-hand page in a book. Have students copy term and definition. Tell briefly of books on display.

> *BOOK SELECTION:* Students return to tables. Have students locate the verso page in their books and check the copyright date. Review frontispiece and verso page. Dismiss by tables. Collect folders.

Lesson 3

SKILL: Knowledge and understanding of the preface, foreword, and introduction.

OBJECTIVE: Students will be introduced to the preface, foreword, and introduction, and be able to locate them in a book.

LITERATURE: Fantasy/seasonal fiction and nonfiction.

PREPARATION: A blank transparency. Overhead projector. Place books containing a preface, foreword, and/or introduction on tables. Display fantasy/seasonal fiction and nonfiction. Place folders on tables.

> *LESSON:* Students take assigned seats. Check attendance. Review frontispiece and verso page. Introduce preface, foreword, and introduction. A preface is an explanation written by the author, a foreword is an introduction written by someone other than the author, and an introduction is written by the author. Have students locate the preface, foreword, and/or introduction in books on table. Have student copy terms and definitions. Tell briefly of books on display.
>
> *BOOK SELECTION:* Students return to tables. Review frontispiece, verso page, and preface, foreword or introduction. Dismiss by tables. Collect folders.

Lesson 4

SKILL: Knowledge and understanding of anthology.

OBJECTIVE: Students will understand that a collection of any type of literature is called an anthology.

LITERATURE: Fantasy/seasonal fiction and nonfiction.

PREPARATION: A blank transparency. Overhead projector. Place a variety of anthologies on tables. Display fantasy/seasonal fiction and nonfiction. Place folders on tables.

LESSON: Students take assigned seats. Check attendance. Using transparency, review frontispiece, verso page, and preface, foreword or introduction. Introduce anthology; a collection of literature. Have students browse through anthologies on tables. Have students copy term and definition from transparency. Tell briefly of books on display.

BOOK SELECTION: Students return to tables. Review frontispiece, verso page, preface, foreword or introduction, and anthology. Dismiss by tables. Collect folders.

JANUARY

Lesson 1

SKILL: Knowledge and understanding of the card catalog.

OBJECTIVE: Students will review their knowledge of the card catalog and the three types of catalog cards.

LITERATURE: Animal fiction and nonfiction.

PREPARATION: Gather together a collection of discarded catalog cards. Band a packet of author, title, and subject cards for each table or group. Make three labels, author, title, and subject. Prepare an introduction to animal fiction and nonfiction. Display animal fiction and nonfiction. Place folders on tables.

LESSON: Students take assigned seats. Check attendance. Review the three kinds of catalog cards. Hand out packets. Students will sort cards into author, title, and subject cards. Check cards, have groups exchange. Introduce animal fiction and nonfiction. Tell briefly of books on display.

BOOK SELECTION: Students return to tables. Review the three kinds of catalog cards. Dismiss by tables. Collect folders.

Lesson 2

SKILL: Knowledge and understanding of the card catalog.

OBJECTIVE: Students will practice decoding the information found on a catalog card.

LITERATURE: Animal fiction and nonfiction.

PREPARATION: A transparency of a set of catalog cards. Overhead projector. At least one copy of the activity "Decoding a Catalog Card" for each student. Discarded catalog cards. Display animal fiction and nonfiction. Place folders on tables.

LESSON: Students take assigned seats. Check attendance. Using transparency, discuss the information found on a catalog card and the location of the information. Hand out activity and cards. Have students complete activity. If there is time, decode more than one card. Tell briefly of books on display.

BOOK SELECTION: Students return to tables. Review author, title, and subject cards and the location of information. Dismiss by tables. Collect folders.

Lesson 3

SKILL: Knowledge and understanding of the card catalog.

OBJECTIVE: Students will be introduced to 'see' and 'see also' references. Students will practice locating books on the shelf.

LITERATURE: Animal fiction and nonfiction.

PREPARATION: Make a transparency of 'see' and 'see also' catalog cards. A copy of the activity "Card Catalog Practice" for each student. A transparency for introduction. Overhead projector. Place one catalog drawer for two students on the tables. Display animal fiction and nonfiction. Place folders on tables.

LESSON: Students take assigned seats. Check attendance. Introduce 'see' and 'see also' references. Hand out activity. Using transparency, introduce activity. Have students complete activity. Tell briefly of books on display.

BOOK SELECTION: Students return to tables. Review lesson. Dismiss by tables. Collect folders.

Lesson 4

SKILL: Knowledge and understanding of the card catalog.

OBJECTIVE: Students will complete an activity designed to review knowledge and understanding of the card catalog.

LITERATURE: Animal fiction and nonfiction.

PREPARATION: A copy of the activity "The Card Catalog Caper" if you use pre-1980 ALA rules or a copy of the activity "A Card Catalog

Caper," if you use 1980 ALA rules for each student. A transparency of activity for introduction. Overhead projector. Display animal fiction and nonfiction. Place folders on tables.

LESSON: Students take assigned seats. Check attendance. Introduce activity. Hand out activity. Have students complete activity. Complete together on transparency. Tell briefly of books on display.

BOOK SELECTION: Students return to tables. Review the card catalog. Dismiss by tables. Collect folders.

Name _____   Date _____

DECODING
A CATALOG CARD

DIRECTIONS: Using a given catalog card, decode the following information.

CALL NUMBER _____

AUTHOR _____

TITLE _____

ILLUSTRATOR _____

PUBLISHER _____

COPYRIGHT DATE _____

NUMBER OF PAGES _____

CIRCLE THE KIND OF CATALOG CARD: AUTHOR   TITLE   SUBJECT

CIRCLE THE TYPE OF BOOK: FICTION   NONFICTION   EASY

Name _____   Date _____

CARD CATALOG PRACTICE

1. Count to the fifth card in the drawer. Using that card, fill in the following information:

   Author _____

   Title _____

   Call Number _____

   Locate the book on the shelf: Book located _____ Book not located _____

2. Select an author card. Using that card, fill in the following information:

   Author _____

   Title _____

   Call Number _____

   Locate the book on the shelf: Book located _____ Book not located _____

3. Select a title card. Using that card, fill in the following information:

   Author _____

   Title _____

   Call Number _____

   Locate the book on the shelf: Book located _____ Book not located _____

4. Select a subject card. Using that card, fill in the following information:

   Author _____

   Title _____

   Call Number _____

   Locate the book on the shelf: Book located _____ Book not located _____

THE CARD CATALOG CAPER

ACROSS

4. St. on the top line of a catalog card is filed as _____.
7. The card catalog is arranged _____.
9. There are _____ main kinds of catalog cards.
11. Mr. on the top line of a catalog card is filed as _____.
12. The author's name appears on a catalog card with the _____ name first.
15. Numbers on the top line of a catalog card are _____ out when filed.
16. The symbol © stands for _____.
19. Catalog cards are arranged in _____.

DOWN

1. The author's name is on the top line of an _____ card.
2. Mrs. is filed in the card catalog as _____.
3. The _____ is located in the upper left corner of a catalog card.
4. The top line is all capital letters on a _____ card.
5. Dr. on the top line of a catalog card is filed as _____.
6. Authors' names beginning with 'Mc' and 'Mac' are filed as _____.
8. The last item on a catalog card is the number of _____.
10. 'A', 'An,' and 'The' on title cards are _____ when filed.
13. One kind of cross-reference is the _____ reference.
14. The other kind of cross-reference is the _____.
17. The card catalog is the _____ to the library's collection.
18. The title is on the top line of a _____ card.

Name _____   Date _____

A CARD CATALOG CAPER

ACROSS

4. The top line is all capital letters on a _____ card.
7. The card catalog is arranged in _____ order.
10. The title is on the top line on a _____ card.
11. A type of cross-reference is the _____ reference.
12. The author's name is on the top line on an _____ card.
14. If the call number contains a number and letters, the book is _____ .
15. If the call number is 921, 92 or B, the book is _____ .

DOWN

1. The company that produces the book is called the _____ .
2. Catalog cards are filed in _____ .
3. The symbol © stands for _____ .
4. One type of cross-reference is called the _____ reference.
5. The _____ is located in the upper left hand corner on a catalog card.
6. The author's name is always _____ name first on a catalog card.
8. If the call number contains only letters, the book is _____ .
9. There are _____ main kinds of catalog cards.
13. The card catalog is the _____ to the library's collection.

FEBRUARY

NOTE: The purpose of February's plan is to introduce the various individual reference books included in the reference collection. Because collections vary and usually contain single copies of these reference works, the lessons can be carried out with one fourth of class using each type of reference work each week.

Lesson 1

SKILL: Knowledge and understanding of author reference books.

OBJECTIVE: Students will practice using author reference works.

LITERATURE: Historical biography.

PREPARATION: Author reference books. A copy of the activity "Author Reference Books" for each student. A transparency for introduction. Overhead projector. Prepare an introduction to biography. Display historical biography.

LESSON: Students take assigned seats. Check attendance. Introduce activity. Hand out materials. Have students complete activity. Collect to correct. Introduce biography. Tell briefly of books on display.

BOOK SELECTION: Students return to tables. Review lesson. Dismiss by tables. Collect folders.

Lesson 2

SKILL: Knowledge and understanding of biographical dictionaries.

OBJECTIVE: Students will practice using biographical dictionaries.

LITERATURE: Historical biography.

PREPARATION: Biographical dictionaries. A copy of the activity, "Biographical Dictionaries" for each student. A transparency for introduction. Overhead projector. Display historical biography.

LESSON: Students take assigned seats. Check attendance. Introduce dictionaries. Hand out activity sheets. Have students complete activity. Tell briefly of books on display.

BOOK SELECTION: Students return to tables. Review lesson. Dismiss by tables. Collect folders.

Lesson 3

SKILL: Knowledge and understanding of gazetteers.

OBJECTIVE: Students will practice using a gazetteer.

LITERATURE: Contemporary biography.

PREPARATION: Gazetteers. A copy of the activity "Gazetteers" for each student. A transparency for introduction. Overhead projector. Display contemporary biography. Place folders on table.

LESSON: Students take assigned seats. Check attendance. Using transparency, introduce gazetteers. Hand out activity. Have students complete activity. Collect to correct. Tell briefly of books on display.

BOOK SELECTION: Students return to tables. Review lesson. Dismiss by tables. Collect folders.

Lesson 4

SKILL: Knowledge and understanding of individual reference books.

OBJECTIVE: Students will be introduced to individual reference books included in the collection.

LITERATURE: Contemporary biography.

PREPARATION: Individual reference books. A copy of the activity, "Individual Reference Books" for each student. A transparency for introduction. Overhead projector. Display contemporary biography. Place folders on tables.

LESSON: Students take assigned seats. Check attendance. Introduce individual reference books, using transparency. Have students fill in title. Have students complete activity. Tell briefly of books on display.

BOOK SELECTION: Students return to tables. Review author reference books, biographical dictionaries, gazetteers, and other individual reference books used.

Name _____   Date _____

AUTHOR REFERENCE BOOKS

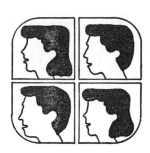

DIRECTIONS: Using an author reference book, complete the following information.

1. Title of reference _____

   Publisher _____

   Copyright Date _____

2. Browse through reference: Length of each article _____ Illustration of Author

   Yes _____   No _____

3. Choose one woman author included in this reference.

   Name _____   Date of Birth _____

   Place of Birth _____   Honors or Awards _____

   Number of Books Written _____

4. Choose one man author included in this reference.

   Name _____   Date of Birth _____

   Place of Birth _____   Honors or Awards _____

   Number of Books Written _____

5. How can author reference books be of help to the reader?

   _____

Name _____   Date _____

BIOGRAPHICAL DICTIONARIES

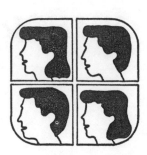

DIRECTIONS: Using a biographical dictionary, complete the following information.

1. Title of reference _____
   Publisher _____
   Copyright Date _____
2. Browse through reference:
   Length of each article _____
   Illustration of person Yes _____ No _____
3. Is this biographical dictionary a general or specialized biography?
   General _____
   Specialized _____
   If specialized, what is the special area? _____
4. Choose a woman included in this biographical dictionary.
   Person _____
   Date of birth _____
   Place of birth _____
   Contribution _____
5. Choose a man included in this biographical dictionary.
   Person _____
   Date of birth _____
   Place of birth _____
   Contribution _____
6. Is copyright date important in biographical dictionaries? Why?

   _____

Name _____   Date _____

GAZETTEERS

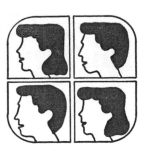

Gazetteers are geographical dictionaries giving names and descriptions of countries, cities, rivers, mountains, and other places in the world.

DIRECTIONS: Using a gazetteer, complete the following information.

1. Title of gazetteer _____
   Publisher _____
   Copyright Date _____
2. What and where is Androscoggin?

   _____

3. What and where is the Lizard?

   _____

4. What four states have counties named Blaine?

   _____

5. What and where is Rum Cay?

   _____

6. What river borders the Catskill Mountains?

   _____

7. What and where is Ross Dependency?

   _____

8. Albuquerque, New Mexico, is located on a river. Name that river.

   _____

Name _____   Date _____

INDIVIDUAL REFERENCE BOOKS

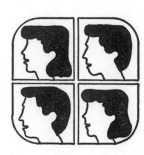

DIRECTIONS: Using the individual reference books available in **your library, complete** the following information.

1. Title _____

   Publisher _____

   Copyright Date _____

   How is this reference of help and interest to the reader?

   _____

   _____

2. Title _____

   Publisher _____

   Copyright Date _____

   How is this reference of help and interest to the reader?

   _____

   _____

3. Title _____

   Publisher _____

   Copyright Date _____

   How is this reference of help and interest to the reader?

   _____

   _____

MARCH

Lesson 1

SKILL: Knowledge and understanding of cross-references.

OBJECTIVE: Students will be introduced to cross-references.

LITERATURE: Science Fiction.

PREPARATION: A copy of the activity "Cross-References" for each student. A transparency for introduction. Overhead projector. Encyclopedias. Prepare an introduction to science fiction. Display science fiction. Place folders on tables.

LESSON: Students take assigned seats. Check attendance. Using transparency, introduce and discuss cross-references. Hand out materials. Have students complete activity. Check activity against encyclopedia volume. Introduce science fiction. Tell briefly of books on display.

BOOK SELECTION: Students return to tables. Review lesson. Dismiss by tables. Collect folders.

Lesson 2

SKILL: Knowledge and understanding of the use of headings.

OBJECTIVE: Students will be introduced to the use of headings in an encyclopedia.

LITERATURE: Science Fiction.

PREPARATION: A copy of the activity "Headings" for each student. A transparency for introduction. Overhead projector. Encyclopedias. Display science fiction. Place folders on tables.

LESSON: Students take assigned seats. Check attendance. Using transparency, introduce and discuss headings. Hand out materials. Have students complete activity. Check against encyclopedia volume. Tell briefly of books on display.

BOOK SELECTION: Students return to tables. Review lesson. Dismiss by tables. Collect folders.

Lesson 3

SKILL: Knowledge and understanding of encyclopedias.

OBJECTIVE: Students will engage in a two-week project designed to afford practice in using encyclopedias.

LITERATURE: Science Fiction.

PREPARATION: A copy of the activity "American Folklore" for each student. A transparency for introduction. Overhead projector. Encyclopedias. Lined paper. Display science fiction. Place folders on tables.

LESSON: Students take assigned seats. Check attendance. Using transparency, introduce project. Decide how many characters students will research. Have students begin activity. Tell briefly of books on display.

BOOK SELECTION: Students return to tables. Discuss progress of project. Dismiss by tables. Collect folders.

Lesson 4

SKILL: Knowledge and understanding of encyclopedias.

OBJECTIVE: Students will complete project designed to afford practice in using encyclopedias.

LITERATURE: Science Fiction.

PREPARATION: Encyclopedias. Lined paper. Plain paper and crayons if you wish to have students illustrate the characters. Display science fiction. Place folders on tables.

LESSON: Students take assigned seats. Check attendance. Review project. Have students complete project. Have students report to class or prepare a bulletin board in library or classroom. Tell briefly of books on display.

BOOK SELECTION: Students return to tables. Review folk tale characters. Dismiss by tables. Collect folders.

Name _____   Date _____

CROSS-REFERENCES

The *"See"* reference is found directly following the key word. The *"See"* reference tells what key word or words to refer to in order to locate the information.

The *"See Also"* reference is found at the end of the article. The *"See Also"* reference suggests other key words to refer to for additional information.

DIRECTIONS: Using a volume of any encyclopedia, answer the following questions.

1. Encyclopedia Title_____

   Volume Number_____

2. Locate *two* examples of *"See"* references.

   A. Key Word_____   "See"_____

   B. Key Word_____   "See"_____

3. Locate *two* examples of *"See Also"* references.

   A. Key Word_____   "See Also"_____

   _____

   _____

   B. Key Word_____   "See Also"_____

   _____

   _____

HEADINGS

HEADINGS divide a long article into sections to assist the reader in locating information quickly. There are two types of headings.

MAIN HEADINGS are printed in dark type. *MAIN HEADINGS* stand alone in the middle of the column.

SUBHEADINGS are printed in dark type. *SUBHEADINGS* are found at the beginning of the article column. *SUBHEADINGS* divide each main section into further sections.

DIRECTIONS: Using a volume of any encyclopedia title:
Locate four *MAIN HEADINGS*
Locate four *SUBHEADINGS*

1. Encyclopedia Title_____

   Volume Number_____

2. *MAIN HEADINGS*   *SUBHEADINGS*

   _____

   _____

   _____

   _____

   _____

   _____

   _____

Name _____   Date _____

AMERICAN FOLKLORE

American Tall Tales are stories and legends in which the truth has been stretched. There is no magic in the tall tales, there is only exaggeration of facts. Some of the American Tall Tales are based on real people, others are based on purely mythological characters.

DIRECTIONS: Choose _____ characters from the following list of tall tale characters. Locate information about the characters in an encyclopedia and write a short report including the information asked for in the questions below.

Tall Tale Characters

Johnny Appleseed	John Henry
Daniel Boone	Jesse James
Paul Bunyan	Casey Jones
Calamity Jane	William Kidd
Kit Carson	Finn Maccool
Davy Crockett	Joe Magarac
Mike Fink	Pecos Bill
Frebold Freboldson	Jim Smiley

The information in the following questions should be included in the report.
1. What is the character's name and nickname?
2. When and where was the character born?
3. Where did the character live?
4. Is the character real or legendary?
5. What were the characteristics of the character?
6. What were the accomplishments of the character?
7. Who were the close friends of the character?
8. Which accomplishments were fact and which were legendary?

APRIL

Lesson 1

SKILL: Knowledge and understanding of the almanac.

OBJECTIVE: Students will be introduced to the almanac.

LITERATURE: Realistic problem-solving fiction and nonfiction.

PREPARATION: One World Almanac for each two students. A copy of the activity "World Almanac Practice 1" for each student. A transparency of activity for introduction. Overhead projector. Prepare an introduction to problem-solving fiction and nonfiction. Display problem-solving fiction and nonfiction. Place folders on tables.

LESSON: Students take assigned seats. Check attendance. Hand out materials. Using transparency, introduce almanacs. Complete activity with the class. Introduce problem-solving fiction and nonfiction. Tell briefly of books on display.

BOOK SELECTION: Students return to tables. Review lesson. Dismiss by tables. Collect folders.

Lesson 2

SKILL: Knowledge and understanding of the almanac.

OBJECTIVE: Students will have practice using an almanac.

LITERATURE: Realistic problem-solving fiction and nonfiction.

PREPARATION: A copy of the activity "World Almanac Practice #2" for each student. A transparency for introduction. One almanac for each two students. Display problem-solving fiction and nonfiction. Place folders on tables.

LESSON: Students take assigned seats. Check attendance. Hand out materials. Using transparency, introduce activity. Have students complete activity. Complete together on transparency. Tell briefly of books on display.

BOOK SELECTION: Students return to tables. Review lesson. Dismiss by tables. Collect folders.

Lesson 3

SKILL: Knowledge and understanding of the almanac.

OBJECTIVE: Students will have practice locating information in the almanac.

LITERATURE: Realistic problem-solving fiction and nonfiction.

PREPARATION: A copy of the activity "World Almanac Practice #3" for each student. A transparency for introduction. Overhead projector. One almanac for each two students. Display problem-solving fiction and nonfiction. Place folders on tables.

LESSON: Students take assigned seats. Check attendance. Hand out materials. Using transparency, introduce activity. Have students complete activity. Complete together on transparency. Tell briefly of books on display.

BOOK SELECTION: Students return to tables. Review lesson. Dismiss by tables. Collect folders.

Lesson 4

SKILL: Knowledge and understanding of the almanac.

OBJECTIVE: Students will have practice locating information in the almanac.

LITERATURE: Realistic problem-solving fiction and nonfiction.

PREPARATION: A copy of activity "World Almanac Practice #4" for each student. A transparency for introduction. Overhead projector. One almanac for each two students. Display problem-solving fiction and nonfiction. Place folders on tables.

LESSON: Students take assigned seats. Check attendance. Hand out materials. Using transparency, introduce activity. Have students complete the activity. Complete activity together on transparency. Tell briefly of books on display.

BOOK SELECTION: Students return to tables. Review lesson. Dismiss by tables. Collect folders.

Name _____   Date _____

WORLD ALMANAC PRACTICE #1

1. What company publishes the World Almanac?

_____

2. Who is the editor of the World Almanac?

_____

3. When was the World Almanac first published?

_____

4. In what month is the World Almanac published today?

_____

5. Where is the index located in the World Almanac?

Front of the book _____ Back of the book _____

6. How is the index to the World Almanac arranged?

Numerically _____ Alphabetically _____

7. Look up the name of your state. Which subtopic would you use to find the origin of the name of your state?

Subtopic_____ Answer_____

8. Look up gasoline. Which subtopic would you choose to find out the cost of the gasoline tax in your state?

Subtopic_____ Answer_____

9. Look up Boston in the index. Which subtopic would you choose to find the name and height of the tallest building in Boston?

Subtopic_____ Answer_____

Name _____   Date _____

WORLD ALMANAC PRACTICE #2

DIRECTIONS: Locate the answers to the following questions.

1. Within what continent is the Ivory Coast located?

   _____

2. Who won baseball's Cy Young Memorial Award in 1963?

   _____

3. Where were the first modern Olympic Games held in 1896?

   _____

4. What is the ancient and modern birthstone for the month of April?

   Ancient _____ Modern _____

5. How many carats are contained in pure gold?

   _____

6. Where was the first atomic bomb produced?

   _____

7. Who was the first prime minister of Canada?

   _____

Name _____   Date _____

WORLD ALMANAC PRACTICE #3

DIRECTIONS: Locate the answers to the following questions.

1. When did the first adhesive postage stamp go on sale?

_____

2. What is the average rise and fall of the tide in Eastport, Maine?

_____

3. What city in North America has the highest altitude?

_____

4. When did government weather agencies begin using female names for hurricanes and tropical storms?

_____

5. Where and when were the first winter Olympic Games held?

_____

6. What is the ancient and modern birthstone for your month?

Birth month _____

Ancient _____ Modern _____

7. In what month and on what day is Citizenship Day celebrated?

_____

Name _____   Date _____

WORLD ALMANAC PRACTICE #4

DIRECTIONS: Locate the answers to the following questions.

1. What province in Canada has the most square miles?

   _____

2. When did government weather agencies begin using male names for hurricanes and tropical storms?

   _____

3. The young of these animals have unusual names. What are they?

   Rooster _____   Swan _____

   Eel _____   Turkey _____

   Kangaroo _____   Hare _____

4. What city in the United States has the highest altitude?

   _____

5. What is the geographical center of mainland USA?

   _____

6. What is the name of the largest island in the world?

   _____

7. What four cities in the United States have the same lowest altitude?

   _____

   _____

   _____

   _____

MAY

Lesson 1

SKILL: Knowledge and understanding of the purpose and format of a bibliography.

OBJECTIVE: Students will be introduced to the purpose of a bibliography. Students will be introduced to the proper form for a bibliography.

LITERATURE: Humorous fiction and nonfiction.

PREPARATION: Prepare an information sheet showing the format for a book, a magazine, and an encyclopedia used in your district. Make a copy for each student. Make a transparency for introduction. Overhead projector. A sheet of lined paper for each student. Place books, magazines, and encyclopedia volumes on tables. Prepare an introduction to humorous fiction and nonfiction. Display humorous fiction and nonfiction. Place folders on tables.

LESSON: Students take assigned seats. Check attendance. Hand out materials. Using transparency, introduce and discuss bibliography. Have students prepare a bibliography for a book, a magazine, and an encyclopedia using the materials on the tables. Introduce humorous fiction and nonfiction. Tell briefly of books on display.

BOOK SELECTION: Students return to tables. Review lesson. Dismiss by tables. Collect folders.

Lesson 2

SKILL: Knowledge and understanding of preparing a bibliography.

OBJECTIVE: Students will practice preparing a bibliography.

LITERATURE: Humorous fiction and nonfiction.

PREPARATION: Transparency of bibliography. Overhead projector. Lined paper. List of subjects. Display humorous fiction and nonfiction. Place folders on tables.

LESSON: Students take assigned seats. Check attendance. Review bibliography. Students will choose subject from list to prepare a bibliography. Students will have three lessons to complete bibliography of books, magazines, encyclopedias, and the like. Tell briefly of books on display.

> *BOOK SELECTION:* Students return to tables. Discuss progress of activity. Dismiss by tables. Collect folders.

Lesson 3

SKILL: Knowledge and understanding of preparing a bibliography.

OBJECTIVE: Students will continue preparing a bibliography.

LITERATURE: Humorous fiction and nonfiction.

PREPARATION: Transparency of bibliography. Overhead projector. Lined paper. Display a selection of humorous fiction and nonfiction.

> *LESSON:* Students take assigned seats. Check attendance. Using transparency, review and discuss bibliography. Have students continue preparing a bibliography on a chosen subject. Tell briefly of books on display.
>
> *BOOK SELECTION:* Students return to tables. Review and discuss progress of activity. Students must complete bibliography during the next lesson. Dismiss by tables. Collect folders.

Lesson 4

SKILL: Knowledge and understanding of preparing a bibliography.

OBJECTIVE: Students will complete the bibliography. Students will put together a class bibliography to be available to all students.

LITERATURE: Humorous fiction and nonfiction.

PREPARATION: A folder for class bibliography. Transparency of bibliography. Overhead projector. Lined paper. Display humorous fiction and nonfiction. Place folders on tables.

> *LESSON:* Students take assigned seats. Check attendance. Using transparency, review progress of activity. Have students complete bibliography. Have students who are finished prepare the folder and a table of contents. Collect bibliographies and place in folder. Have folder available to all students in the library. Tell briefly of books on display.
>
> *BOOK SELECTION:* Students return to tables. Review and discuss results of the project. Dismiss by tables. Collect folders.

JUNE

Lesson 1

SKILL: Knowledge and understanding of choosing the proper reference source.

OBJECTIVE: Students will review and reinforce their skills in choosing the proper reference source.

LITERATURE: Fiction and nonfiction with foreign setting.

PREPARATION: A copy of the activity "Reference Quest" for each student. A transparency for introduction. Overhead projector. Prepare an introduction to fiction and nonfiction with foreign setting. Display a selection of genre. Place folders on tables.

LESSON: Students take assigned seats. Check attendance. Hand out activity. Using transparency, introduce activity. Have students complete activity. Collect to correct. Introduce fiction and nonfiction with foreign setting. Tell briefly of books on display.

BOOK SELECTION: Students return to tables. Review lesson. Dismiss by tables. Collect folders.

Lesson 2

SKILL: Knowledge and understanding of choosing the proper reference source.

OBJECTIVE: Students will review and reinforce their skills in choosing the proper reference source.

LITERATURE: Fiction and nonfiction with foreign setting.

PREPARATION: Activity sheets corrected. Transparency of activity. Overhead projector. Display fiction and nonfiction with foreign setting. Place folders on tables.

LESSON: Students take assigned seats. Check attendance. Hand back activity. Using transparency, go over activity. Discuss and reinforce weak areas. Tell briefly of books on display.

BOOK SELECTION: Students return to tables. Review lesson. Dismiss by tables. Collect folders.

Lesson 3

SKILL: Knowledge and appreciation of literature.

OBJECTIVE: Students will become aware of the literature tastes of the class.

LITERATURE: Fiction and nonfiction with foreign setting.

PREPARATION: A copy of the activity sheet "Literature # 1" for each student. A transparency for introduction. Overhead projector. Student reading records. Display fiction and nonfiction with foreign setting. Place folders on tables.

LESSON: Students take assigned seats. Check attendance. Using transparency, introduce activity. Students will use their own reading records to complete activity. Have students share answers with class. Tell briefly of books on display.

BOOK SELECTION: Students return to tables. Review lesson. Dismiss by tables. Collect folders.

Lesson 4

SKILL: Appreciation and knowledge of literature.

OBJECTIVE: Students will understand and appreciate individual tastes in literature.

LITERATURE: As this is the last lesson, there will be no book selection.

PREPARATION: A copy of the activity sheet "Literature # 2" for each student. A transparency for introduction. Drawing paper. Crayons. Place folders on tables.

LESSON: Students take assigned seats. Check attendance. Hand out materials. Using transparency, introduce activity. Have students complete activity. The drawings make an excellent bulletin board for summer book selection or to use for next September. Have each student count number of books read and recorded this year. Have a total number count for individual, table, and class. Discuss any summer reading programs available for students. Folders go home with students. Dismiss by tables.

Name _____   Date _____

REFERENCE QUEST

DIRECTIONS: Below you will find a list of reference tools. Which tool would be the best choice to locate the answers to the questions below?

ALMANAC   BIOGRAPHICAL DICTIONARY
ATLAS   CARD CATALOG
AUTHOR BOOKS   ENCYCLOPEDIA
          GAZETTEER

1. _____ The salary of the president of the United States.

2. _____ The number of pages in the book *Charlotte's Web.*

3. _____ Where and when Judy Blume was born.

4. _____ A map of Switzerland.

5. _____ The eating habits of mice.

6. _____ How many states have counties named Blaine?

7. _____ The illustrator of the book *Dear Mr. Henshaw.*

8. _____ How the United States ranks in the production of oil.

9. _____ Where Dr. Seuss went to college.

10. _____ The birthplace of Melvil Dewey.

11. _____ How paper is made.

12. _____ The decathlon winner in the most recent Olympic games.

13. _____ The mountain range of which Mount Blackburn is a part.

14. _____ The number of schools in your state.

15. _____ The number of books on snakes in your library.

Name _____   Date _____

LITERATURE! #1

DIRECTIONS: Using your own bibliography of books read and recorded, fill in the sheet.

1. Number of books read _____

2. My favorite: Author   Title

   Family-school book _____

   Mystery or detective book _____

   Historical book _____

   Animal book _____

   Fantasy _____

   Biography _____

   Science fiction book _____

   Humorous book _____

   Foreign setting book _____

3. The best book I read this year _____

4. The longest book I read this year _____

5. The shortest book I read this year _____

6. My favorite author this year _____

7. My favorite kind of book this year _____

Name _____   Date _____

LITERATURE! #2

The most popular books in our class this year.

Author   Title

_____   _____

_____   _____

_____   _____

_____   _____

_____   _____

Books I recommend for summer reading.

Author   Title

_____   _____

_____   _____

_____   _____

_____   _____

_____   _____

Draw an original book jacket for your favorite book read this year.

GRADE 5

OVERVIEW

The main objectives in fifth grade are:
- to correlate the skills closely with the classroom curriculum.
- to continue to introduce and reinforce parts of the book and the story.
- to introduce the Newbery Award collection.
- to introduce and reinforce the skill of outlining and taking notes.
- to reinforce card catalog skills.
- to reinforce knowledge of the Dewey Decimal Classification System.
- to introduce the purpose of the vertical file.
- to introduce the Readers' Guide.
- to continue to introduce various genres to continue to develop students' interest areas.

Students will record books read each week. Students will bring books to tables, record titles read, and return the books to the returning books truck. Attendance will be taken during this time.

Literature-Monthly Genres

Newbery Award
Family-School
Mystery-Detective
Historical
Fantasy
Seasonal

Animal
Biography
Science Fiction
Humorous
Foreign Setting

SEPTEMBER

Lesson 1

SKILL: Knowledge and understanding of library procedures and location of materials in the library.

OBJECTIVE: Students will review library regulations and location of materials.

LITERATURE: Family and school fiction and nonfiction.

PREPARATION: A map of your facility. Number each area. List the areas at the bottom followed by a blank line. A copy for each student. A transparency for introduction. Overhead projector. Materials for folders. Prepare an introduction to family and school fiction and nonfiction. Display books on genre. Class roster. A 4 × 6 sheet for table number.

LESSON: Students sit where they wish. Check attendance. Hand out activity sheet. Using transparency, introduce activity. Students will label the parts of the library. Correct together, using transparency. Hand out materials for folders. Introduce genre. Tell briefly of books on display.

BOOK SELECTION: Students return to tables. Review lesson. Dismiss by tables. Collect folders.

Lesson 2

SKILL: Knowledge and understanding of the Newbery Award.

OBJECTIVE: Students will be introduced to the Newbery Award.

LITERATURE: Newbery Award books.

PREPARATION: A copy of the "Newbery Award Winners," "Newbery Award Books I've Read," and "The Newbery Story" for each student. Transparencies for introduction. Overhead projector. Prepare seating plan. Folders to pass out. Display Newbery Award books.

LESSON: Assign seating. Check attendance. Hand out folders. Hand out all materials. Introduce the Newbery Award collection. Tell briefly of as many books as possible.

BOOK SELECTION: Students return to tables. Review lesson. Have students put folders in middle of table with table number sheet on top. Dismiss by tables. Collect folders.

Lesson 3

SKILL: Knowledge and understanding of the parts of the book.

OBJECTIVE: Students will review the parts of the book. Students will be introduced to the appendix.

LITERATURE: Family and school fiction and nonfiction.

PREPARATION: A copy of the "Parts of the Book" activity for each student. A transparency for introduction. A blank transparency. Overhead projector. Display family and school fiction and nonfiction. Place folders on tables.

LESSON: Students take assigned seats. Check attendance. Using blank transparency, review the parts of the book. Introduce appendix. Hand out activity. Introduce activity. Have students complete activity. Collect to correct and/or complete activity on transparency. Tell briefly of books on display.

BOOK SELECTION: Students return to tables. Review lesson. Dismiss by tables. Collect folders.

Lesson 4

SKILL: Knowledge and understanding of the concepts and parts of the story.

OBJECTIVE: Students will review the concepts and parts of the story. Students will be introduced to these and genre.

LITERATURE: Family and school fiction and nonfiction.

PREPARATION: A copy of the activity "Concepts and Parts of the Story" for each student. A transparency for introduction. A blank transparency. Overhead projector. Display family and school fiction and nonfiction. Place folders on tables.

LESSON: Students take assigned seats. Check attendance. Using blank transparency, review the concepts and parts of the story. Introduce theme and genre. Hand out activity sheets. Introduce activity. Have students complete activity. Complete activity together on transparency. Tell briefly of books on display.

BOOK SELECTION: Students return to tables. Review lesson. Dismiss by tables. Collect folders.

NEWBERY GOLD MEDAL WINNERS

1922	Van Loon, Hendrik Willem. *The Story of Mankind.*
1923	Lofting, Hugh. *The Voyages of Doctor Dolittle.*
1924	Hawes, Charles. *The Dark Frigate.*
1925	Finger, Charles. *Tales from Silver Lands.*
1926	Chrisman, Arthur Bowie. *Shen of the Sea.*
1927	James, Will. *Smoky the Cowhorse.*
1928	Mukerji, Dhan Gopal. *Gay-Neck, The Story of a Pigeon.*
1929	Kelly, Eric P. *The Trumpeter of Krakow.*
1930	Field, Rachel. *Hitty, Her First Hundred Years.*
1931	Coatsworth, Elizabeth. *The Cat Who Went to Heaven.*
1932	Armer, Laura Adams. *Waterless Mountain.*
1933	Lewis, Elizabeth Foreman. *Young Fu of the Upper Yangtze.*
1934	Meigs, Cornelia. *Invincible Louisa.*
1935	Shannon, Monica. *Dobry.*
1936	Brink, Carol Ryrie. *Caddie Woodlawn.*
1937	Sawyer, Ruth. *Roller Skates.*
1938	Seredy, Kate. *The White Stag.*
1939	Enright, Elizabeth. *Thimble Summer.*
1940	Daugherty, James. *Daniel Boone.*
1941	Sperry, Armstrong. *Call It Courage.*
1942	Edmonds, Walter. *The Matchlock Gun.*
1943	Gray, Elizabeth Gray. *Adam of the Road.*
1944	Forbes, Esther. *Johnny Tremain.*
1945	Lawson, Robert. *Rabbit Hill.*
1946	Lenski, Lois. *Strawberry Girl.*
1947	Bailey, Carolyn Sherwin. *Miss Hickory.*
1948	Du Bois, William Pene. *The Twenty-One Balloons.*
1949	Henry, Marguerite. *King of the Wind.*

NEWBERY GOLD MEDAL WINNERS (continued)

1950   De Angeli, Marguerite. *The Door in the Wall.*

1951   Yates, Elizabeth. *Amos Fortune, Free Man.*

1952   Estes, Eleanor. *Ginger Pye.*

1953   Clark, Ann Nolan. *Secret of the Andes.*

1954   Krumgold, Joseph. *And Now Miguel.*

1955   De Jong, Meindert. *The Wheel on the School.*

1956   Latham, Jean Lee. *Carry On, Mr. Bowditch.*

1957   Sorensen, Virginia. *Miracles on Maple Hill.*

1958   Keith, Harold. *Rifles for Watie.*

1959   Speare, Elizabeth. *The Witch of Black-bird Pond.*

1960   Krumgold, Joseph. *Onion John.*

1961   O'Dell, Scott. *Island of the Blue Dolphins.*

1962   Speare, Elizabeth. *The Bronze Bow.*

1963   L'Engle, Madeleine. *A Wrinkle in Time.*

1964   Neville, Emily. *It's Like This, Cat.*

1965   Wojciechowska, Maia. *Shadow of a Bull.*

1966   De Trevino, Elizabeth Borton. *I, Juan de Pareja.*

1967   Hunt, Irene. *Up a Road Slowly.*

1968   Konigsburg, Elaine. *From the Mixed-Up Files of Mrs. Basil E. Frankweiler.*

1969   Alexander, Lloyd. *The High King.*

1970   Armstrong, William. *Sounder.*

1971   Byars, Betsy. *Summer of the Swans.*

1972   O'Brien, Robert C. *Mrs. Frisby and the Rats of NIMH.*

1973   George, Jean. *Julie of the Wolves.*

1974   Fox, Paula. *The Slave Dancer.*

1975   Hamilton, Virginia. *M. C. Higgins the Great.*

1976   Cooper, Susan. *The Grey King.*

1977   Taylor, Mildred. *Roll of Thunder, Hear My Cry.*

NEWBERY GOLD MEDAL WINNERS (continued)

1978	Paterson, Katherine. *Bridge to Terabithia.*
1979	Raskin, Ellen. *The Westing Game.*
1980	Blos, Joan. *A Gathering of Days: A New England's Girl Journal, 1830-1832.*
1981	Paterson, Katherine. *Jacob Have I Loved.*
1982	Willard, Nancy. *A Visit to William Blake's Inn: Poems for Innocent and Experienced Travelers.*
1983	Voigt, Cynthia. *Dicey's Song.*
1984	Cleary, Beverly. *Dear Mr. Henshaw.*
1985	McKinley, Robin. *The Hero and the Crown.*
1986	MacLachlan, Patricia. *Sarah, Plain and Tall.*
1987	Fleischman. *The Whipping Boy.*

Name _____ Date _____

NEWBERY AWARD BOOKS I'VE READ

Date	Author	Title

Name _____   Date _____

THE NEWBERY STORY

John Newbery was born in Berkshire, England in 1713. John's father was a farmer and expected his son to become a farmer, as it was customary in those days for a son to follow in his father's work.

John did not want to become a farmer, however, and in 1744 he moved to London. He opened a bookstore and patent medicine shop called the *Bible and Sun.*

John was always thinking of ways to increase business. One day, a notice appeared in the window announcing a special book for children. A picture book, *A Little Pretty Pocket Book,* was displayed next to the notice. This was the first book to be written and illustrated just for children. The book was a great success. John Newbery published more than twenty books for children during his lifetime.

During the American Library Association's annual meeting in Swampscott, Massachusetts, on June 21, 1921, Frederic Melcher, secretary of the American Booksellers Association, surprised the librarians by proposing that an award be established for excellence in children's literature. After careful consideration, the librarians voted to accept Melcher's proposal and his further suggestion that the award be named in honor of John Newbery.

The American Library Association passed a resolution in 1922, that a bronze medal be awarded annually to the author of "The most distinguished contribution to American literature for children" published during the preceding year. The only limits placed on the award were that the author must be a citizen or resident of the United States and that the work must be original. No retellings or compilations would be considered.

The first Newbery Medal was awarded in 1922 to Hendrik Willem Van Loon for his book, *The Story of Mankind.* Today, a committee of the Children's Service division of the American Library Association selects the winner. The announcement is made at the midwinter meeting of the American Library Association.

Although the award carries no monetary value, this prestigious award brings fame to the author and assures financial gain through the large volume of sales of the book.

Name _____   Date _____

PARTS OF THE BOOK

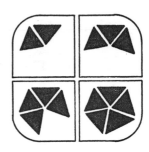

DIRECTIONS: The parts of the book are listed below. Match up the part with the definition by writing the part on the blank line.

APPENDIX	INDEX
BIBLIOGRAPHY	PAGES
BOOK OR DUST JACKET	PREFACE OR FOREWORD
COVER	SPINE
DEDICATION PAGE	TABLE OF CONTENTS
FRONTISPIECE	TITLE PAGE
GLOSSARY	VERSO PAGE

1. _____ The page on which the author thanks a person or persons as a mark of affection or gratitude.

2. _____ A picture opposite the title page.

3. _____ The "business page" of the book containing the title, author, illustrator, publisher, and place of publication.

4. _____ A list of definitions of special words in a book.

5. _____ A list of other materials on a particular subject.

6. _____ A paper cover that protects the spine and cover.

7. _____ The back of the title page, called the copyright page.

8. _____ The written introduction to a book.

9. _____ The page listing the chapters and page numbers.

10. _____ The backbone of the book.

11. _____ The sheets or leaves of paper in a book.

12. _____ The boards that bind the cover to the spine.

13. _____ A list of subjects and page numbers in the back of the book.

14. _____ A section at the back of the book containing extra or supportive material.

Name _____   Date _____

CONCEPTS AND PARTS OF THE STORY

DIRECTIONS: The concepts and parts of the story are listed below. Write the answer to the definition on the blank line.

ACTION
AUTHOR
BEGINNING OF STORY
COPYRIGHT DATE
DESCRIPTION
DIALOGUE
END OF STORY
GENRE
ILLUSTRATIONS

ILLUSTRATOR
MAIN CHARACTER
MIDDLE OF STORY
PLOT
PUBLISHER
SETTING
SUPPORTING
CHARACTERS
THEME
TITLE

1. _____ The conversation of the characters in the story.
2. _____ Whoever is most important in the story.
3. _____ The pictures in the story.
4. _____ The person who wrote the story.
5. _____ Where the story takes place.
6. _____ The message of the story.
7. _____ The name of the story.
8. _____ Others of importance in the story.
9. _____ The introduction part of the story.
10. _____ The company that prints and sells the book.
11. _____ The dramatic events that moves the story along.
12. _____ The kind, type, or category of story.
13. _____ The person who created the pictures for the story.
14. _____ The date the story was published.
15. _____ The part of the story where most of the action occurs.
16. _____ The plan of the story, or what the story is all about.
17. _____ The wrap-up part of the story.
18. _____ Detail used to create a visual image for the reader.

OCTOBER

Lesson 1

SKILL: Knowledge and understanding of outlining.

OBJECTIVE: Students will practice outlining.

LITERATURE: Mystery and detective fiction and nonfiction. Newbery mystery and detective fiction.

PREPARATION: A copy of "The Newbery Story" (in students' folders). Lined paper for each student. A blank transparency. Overhead projector. Prepare an introduction to mystery and detective fiction and nonfiction. Display mystery and detective fiction and nonfiction. Place folders on tables.

LESSON: Students take assigned seats. Check attendance. Using "The Newbery Story," prepare an outline on transparency with the students. Have students copy the outline. Introduce mystery and detective fiction and nonfiction. Tell briefly of books on display.

BOOK SELECTION: Students return to tables. Review lesson. Dismiss by tables. Collect folders.

Lesson 2

SKILL: Knowledge and understanding of paraphrasing.

OBJECTIVE: Students will practice paraphrasing.

LITERATURE: Mystery and detective fiction and nonfiction.

PREPARATION: Students' outline from last lesson. Transparency of outline. Overhead projector. Lined paper for each student. Display mystery and detective fiction and nonfiction. Place folders on tables.

LESSON: Students take assigned seats. Check attendance. Discuss paraphrasing. Review outline of "The Newbery Story." Have students rewrite "The Newbery Story" using the outline. Compare with the original as an example of paraphrasing. Tell briefly of books on display.

BOOK SELECTION: Students return to tables. Review lesson. Dismiss by tables. Collect folders.

Lesson 3

SKILL: Knowledge and understanding of taking notes.

OBJECTIVE: Students will practice taking notes in outline form.

LITERATURE: Mystery and detective fiction and nonfiction.

PREPARATION: An encyclopedia volume for each student. Lined paper for each student. A blank transparency. Overhead projector. Display mystery and detective fiction and nonfiction. Place folders on tables.

LESSON: Students take assigned seats. Check attendance. Introduce and discuss taking notes. Using transparency, write "early life," "adult life," and "contributions." Have students look up any person in an encyclopedia. Students are to read and take notes on that person. Using notes, students will write a short report on the person. Tell briefly of books on display.

BOOK SELECTION: Students return to tables. Review lesson. Dismiss by tables. Collect folders.

Lesson 4

SKILL: Knowledge and understanding of preparing a bibliography.

OBJECTIVE: Students will review preparing a bibliography.

LITERATURE: Mystery and detective fiction and nonfiction.

PREPARATION: A copy of the bibliography form used in your district. An encyclopedia, a magazine, and a book for each student. Lined paper. A blank transparency. Overhead projector. Display mystery and detective fiction and nonfiction. Place folders on tables.

LESSON: Students take assigned seats. Check attendance. Review the form for bibliography. Write examples on transparency. Have students prepare a bibliography using the encyclopedias, magazines, and books on tables. Check progress. Tell briefly of books on display.

BOOK SELECTION: Students return to tables. Review lesson. Dismiss by tables. Collect folders.

NOVEMBER

As most libraries do not have multiple copies of the following reference tools, November's lessons may be planned to run simultaneously as learning stations, with one-fourth of the class covering each reference tool each week.

Lesson 1

SKILL: Knowledge and understanding of biographical dictionaries.

OBJECTIVE: Students will review and reinforce the skills in using biographical dictionaries.

LITERATURE: Historical fiction and nonfiction. Newbery historical fiction and nonfiction.

PREPARATION: Biographical dictionaries. A copy of the activity "Biographical Dictionaries" for each student. A transparency for introduction. Overhead projector. Lined paper for each student. Prepare an introduction to historical fiction and nonfiction. Display books on the genre. Place folders on tables.

LESSON: Students take assigned seats. Check attendance. Using transparency, introduce activity. Have students complete activity. Introduce genre. Tell briefly of books on display.

BOOK SELECTION: Students return to tables. Review lesson. Dismiss by tables. Collect folders.

Lesson 2

SKILL: Knowledge and understanding of gazetteers/geographical dictionaries.

OBJECTIVE: Students will review and reinforce their skills using gazetteers/ geographical dictionaries.

LITERATURE: Historical fiction and nonfiction.

PREPARATION: Gazetteers. A copy of "Practice Using Gazetteers or Geographical Dictionaries." A transparency to introduce activity. Overhead projector. Display historical fiction and nonfiction. Place folders on tables.

LESSON: Students take assigned seats. Check attendance. Introduce activity. Have students complete activity. Tell briefly of books on display.

BOOK SELECTION: Students return to tables. Review lesson. Dismiss by tables. Collect folders.

Lesson 3

SKILL: Knowledge and understanding of author reference books.

OBJECTIVE: Students will review and reinforce their skills using author reference books.

LITERATURE: Historical fiction and nonfiction.

PREPARATION: A copy of "Practice Using Author Reference Books" for each student. A transparency for introduction. Overhead projector. Display historical fiction and nonfiction. Place folders on tables.

LESSON: Students take assigned seats. Check attendance. Using transparency, introduce activity. Have students complete activity. Tell briefly of books on display.

BOOK SELECTION: Students return to tables. Review lesson. Dismiss by tables. Collect folders.

Lesson 4

SKILL: Knowledge and understanding of the vertical file.

OBJECTIVE: Students will be introduced to the vertical file and will have practice using the vertical file.

LITERATURE: Historical fiction and nonfiction.

PREPARATION: A copy of "The Vertical File" for each student. Vertical file. A transparency for introduction. Overhead projector. Display historical fiction and nonfiction. Place folders on tables.

LESSON: Students take assigned seats. Check attendance. Introduce activity. Have students complete activity. Tell briefly of books on display.

BOOK SELECTION: Students return to tables. Review lesson. Dismiss by tables. Collect folders.

PRACTICE USING A GAZETTEER OR GEOGRAPHICAL DICTIONARY

Gazetteers or geographical dictionaries contain names, locations, and descriptions of countries, cities, mountains, rivers, and other physical features of places.

DIRECTIONS: Using a gazetteer or geographical dictionary, answer the following questions.

1. What and where is Alert Bay?

   _____

2. What is the location of Dunk Island?

   _____

3. What and where is Acoma?

   _____

4. What and where is Germiston?

   _____

5. How many islands are in the Ionian Islands? Where are they located?

   _____

   _____

Name _____   Date _____

BIOGRAPHICAL DICTIONARIES

Biographical dictionaries contain short, concise entries about noteworthy people.

DIRECTIONS: Choose _____ people from the names listed below. Using a biographical dictionary, write a short report on each person, including the information asked for below.

© 1988 by The Center for Applied Research in Education

_____ HENRI BOURASSA   _____ KING PHILIP

_____ ETIENNE BRULE   _____ AGNES MACPHAIL

_____ JACQUES CARTIER   _____ LOUIS J. PAPINEAU

_____ VIRGINIA DARE   _____ LAURA SECORD

_____ MARY DYER   _____ SAMUEL SEWALL

_____ PETER FANEUIL   _____ PETER STUYVESANT

Information to be included:

1. When and where the person was born.

2. Where the person spent his/her adult life.

3. The occupation or profession of the person.

4. Where and when the person accomplished the contributions for which the person is remembered.

5. Where and when the person died.

Name _____   Date _____

PRACTICE USING AUTHOR REFERENCE BOOKS

Author reference books give information concerning the lives of authors

DIRECTIONS: Choose _____ authors from the names listed below. Using an author reference book, write a short report on each author, including the information asked for below.

_____ LLOYD ALEXANDER   _____ VIRGINIA HAMILTON

_____ BETSY BYARS   _____ ROBERT LAWSON

_____ BEVERLY CLEARY   _____ MADELINE L'ENGLE

_____ MEINDERT DE JONG   _____ KATHERINE PATERSON

_____ JEAN GEORGE   _____ MILDRED TAYLOR

Information to be included:

1. When and where the author was born.

2. When and why did the author begin writing.

3. When was the author's first book published?

4. What awards has the author won?

5. How many books has the author written? How many have you read?

Name _____   Date _____

THE VERTICAL FILE

The vertical file contains information in the form of pictures, brochures, booklets, and clippings and articles from newspapers, magazines, and other sources.

DIRECTIONS: Using the vertical file answer the following questions.

1. Does your vertical file have information on the following subjects.
   a. ANIMALS   Yes ____   No ____
   b. HOLIDAYS   Yes ____   No ____
   c. ITALY   Yes ____   No ____
   d. JAPAN   Yes ____   No ____

2. Name your state _____

   a. Is there material on your state?   Yes ____   No ____
   b. Is there material on your city or town?   Yes ____   No ____

3. May you borrow materials from the vertical file?   Yes ____   No ____
   a. If you may, describe the check-out process.

   _____
   _____
   _____

4. May students contribute to the vertical file in your library?   Yes ____   No ____
   a. If you may, describe the process.

   _____
   _____
   _____

A-G
H-M
N-R
S-Z

DECEMBER

Lesson 1

SKILL: Comparison of information in encyclopedias.

OBJECTIVE: Students will compare strengths of various encyclopedias.

LITERATURE: Fantasy. Newbery fantasy. Seasonal fiction and nonfiction.

PREPARATION: Encyclopedias. A copy of "Comparison of Information in Encyclopedias #1." A transparency for introduction. Overhead projector. Prepare an introduction to the genres. Display books on genre.

LESSON: Students take assigned seats. Check attendance. Hand out activity. Review why more than one encyclopedia should be checked. Using transparency, introduce activity. Have students complete part one of activity. Introduce fantasy and/or seasonal fiction and nonfiction. Tell briefly of books on display.

BOOK SELECTION: Students return to tables. Review lesson. Dismiss by tables. Collect folders.

Lesson 2

SKILL: Comparison of information in encyclopedias.

OBJECTIVE: Students will compare strengths of encyclopedias.

LITERATURE: Fantasy. Seasonal fiction and nonfiction.

PREPARATION: Encyclopedias. A copy of "Comparison of Information in Encyclopedias #2" for each table or group. A transparency for introduction. Overhead projector. Place the same letter volume of each encyclopedia title on each table. Display books on the genres. Place folders on tables.

LESSON: Students take assigned seats. Check attendance. Have students complete parts 2 and 3 of last week's activity. Using transparency, introduce today's activity. Have students begin activity which will be completed next week. Tell briefly of books on display.

BOOK SELECTION: Students return to tables. Review lesson. Dismiss by tables. Collect folders.

Lesson 3

SKILL: Comparison of information in encyclopedias.

OBJECTIVE: Students will compare strengths of various encyclopedias.

LITERATURE: Fantasy. Seasonal fiction and nonfiction.

PREPARATION: Transparency of last week's activity. Overhead projector. Place encyclopedias on tables. Display books on genre. Place folders on tables.

LESSON: Students take assigned seats. Check attendance. Using transparency, review activity started last week. Have students continue and complete activity. Tell briefly of books on display.

BOOK SELECTION: Students return to tables. Review lesson. Dismiss by tables. Collect folders.

Lesson 4

SKILL: Comparison of information in encyclopedias.

OBJECTIVE: Students will compare strengths of various encyclopedias.

LITERATURE: Fantasy. Seasonal fiction and nonfiction.

PREPARATION: A copy of "Comparison of Information in Encyclopedias — An Opinion Poll" for each student. A transparency of activity. Overhead projector. Display books on the genres. Place folders on tables.

LESSON: Students take assigned seats. Check attendance. Using transparency, have each group give a topic and complete activity. Discuss the results and draw conclusions. Tell briefly of books on display.

BOOK SELECTION: Students return to tables. Review lesson and unit. Dismiss by tables. Collect folders.

Name _____   Date _____

COMPARISON OF INFORMATION IN ENCYCLOPEDIAS #1

DIRECTIONS: List below the encyclopedia titles available in your library.

Title of Encyclopedia	*Latest copyright date*
1. _____	_____
2. _____	_____
3. _____	_____
4. _____	_____
5. _____	_____
6. _____	_____
7. _____	_____

Your table or group will be assigned a letter or group of letters to compare in each encyclopedia. Be careful to look at the same letter in each encyclopedia, even if it means you have to use more than one volume.

Each person in the group will choose a topic beginning with the letter included in your volumes. The group will compare the information in each title and write its opinion on Part 2 of the activity.

Topic	Person
1. _____	_____
2. _____	_____
3. _____	_____
_____	_____

Name _____   Date _____

COMPARISON OF INFORMATION IN ENCYCLOPEDIAS #2

DIRECTIONS: The group will check the topic chosen by each person in each encyclopedia. In the opinion of the group, which title gives the best information? Defend your answer.

1. TOPIC _____

    Title Chosen _____

    Why _____

    _____

2. TOPIC _____

    Title Chosen _____

    Why _____

    _____

3. TOPIC _____

    Title Chosen _____

    Why _____

    _____

4. TOPIC _____

    Title Chosen _____

    Why _____

    _____

COMPARISON OF INFORMATION IN ENCYCLOPEDIAS—AN OPINION POLL

DIRECTIONS: Each group will present a topic and tell which encyclopedia they think covers it best. On the form below, write in the topic and put a checkmark (√) under the title of the encyclopedia chosen. When each group has given a presentation, discuss the results and draw conclusions.

TOPIC	TITLE	TITLE	TITLE	TITLE	TITLE	TITLE

JANUARY

Lesson 1

SKILL: Knowledge and understanding of the card catalog.

OBJECTIVE: Students will complete a test designed to determine mastery of the use of the card catalog.

LITERATURE: Animal fiction and nonfiction. Newbery animal fiction.

PREPARATION: A copy of "Card Catalog Review" for each student. A transparency for introduction. Overhead projector. Prepare an introduction to animal fiction and nonfiction. Display animal fiction and nonfiction. Place folders on tables.

LESSON: Students take assigned seats. Hand out activity. Using transparency, introduce test. Have students complete test. Collect to correct. Complete test as class activity on transparency. Introduce animal fiction and nonfiction. Tell briefly of books on display.

BOOK SELECTION: Students return to tables. Review lesson. Dismiss by tables. Collect folders.

Lesson 2

SKILL: Knowledge and understanding of the card catalog.

OBJECTIVE: Students will review test results. Students will review their knowledge of the "inside guides" of the card catalog.

LITERATURE: Animal fiction and nonfiction.

PREPARATION: Test corrected. Transparency of test. A copy of "The Card Catalog 'Inside Guides'" for each student. A transparency for introduction. Overhead projector. Display animal fiction and nonfiction. Place folders on tables.

LESSON: Students take assigned seats. Check attendance. Hand back tests. Go over test with students using transparency. Introduce the "inside guides." Have students complete activity. Tell briefly of books on display.

BOOK SELECTION: Students return to tables. Review lesson. Dismiss by tables. Collect folders.

Lesson 3

SKILL: Knowledge and understanding of the card catalog.

OBJECTIVE: Students will complete a word search puzzle based on the card catalog.

LITERATURE: Animal fiction and nonfiction.

PREPARATION: A copy of "Card Catalog Wordsearch" for each student. A transparency for introduction. Overhead projector. Display animal fiction and nonfiction. Place folders on tables.

LESSON: Students take assigned seats. Check attendance. Using transparency, introduce activity. Have students complete activity. Complete activity with class on transparency. Tell briefly of books on display.

BOOK SELECTION: Students return to tables. Review lesson. Dismiss by tables. Collect folders.

Lesson 4

SKILL: Knowledge and understanding of the card catalog.

OBJECTIVE: Students will reinforce card catalog skills.

LITERATURE: Animal fiction and nonfiction.

PREPARATION: There is a choice of lesson here. Using materials of your choice, bolster any area card catalog skills that seem to be weak, or use media as a final review to the unit. Display animal fiction and nonfiction. Place folders on tables.

LESSON: Students take assigned seats. Check attendance. Introduce lesson. Complete lesson. Tell briefly of books on display.

BOOK SELECTION: Students return to tables. Review lesson. Dismiss by tables. Collect folders.

Name _____   Date _____

CARD CATALOG REVIEW

DIRECTIONS: Fill in the blanks.

1. The three main kinds of catalog cards are:

   a. _____

   b. _____

   c. _____

2. Name *seven* items found on a catalog card.

   a. _____

   b. _____

   c. _____

   d. _____

   e. _____

   f. _____

   g. _____

DIRECTIONS: Fill in the answer on the blank line.

3. The card catalog is arranged _____

4. On an author card, the _____

   is printed on the top line.

5. On a title card, the _____

   is printed on the top line.

CARD CATALOG REVIEW (continued)

DIRECTIONS: Fill in the answer on the blank line.

6. On a subject card, the ——————————————— is printed on the top line.

7. The card catalog consists of cards arranged in wooden, plastic, or metal ————
——————————————————————————— .

8. Author cards are filed in the card catalog with the author's —————————
name first.

9. The call number is located in the ———————————————————
of a catalog card.

10. The card catalog is the ——————————————— to the library's collection.

DIRECTIONS: Circle the correct answer.

11. If the call number consists of a number with a letter or letters directly beneath
the number, the book is:

    a. Fiction   b. Nonfiction

12. If the call number consists of a letter or letters, the book is:

    a. Fiction   b. Nonfiction

13. *A, an,* and *the* at the beginning of a title are not used when alphabetizing a title
card.

    a. True   b. False

14. If two or more authors have the same last name, the author cards are filed
alphabetically by the first name.

    a. True   b. False

15. If an author has written two or more books, the author cards are filed alphabetically first by author then by title.

    a. True   b. False

THE CARD CATALOG "INSIDE GUIDES"

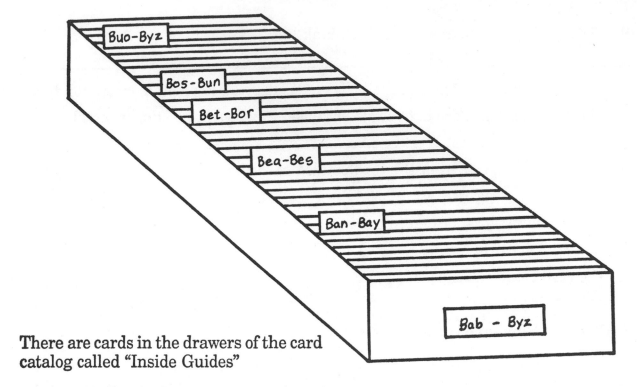

There are cards in the drawers of the card catalog called "Inside Guides"

"Inside Guides" stand higher than the catalog cards.

"Inside Guides" divide each drawer into alphabetical sections.

"Inside Guides" help you locate the section of the drawer in which the card you are looking for is located, without having to go card by card from the beginning of the drawer.

DIRECTIONS: If you were looking for the following authors, titles, or subjects, after which guide card would you check?

1. James Barrie _____
2. Black Beauty _____
3. BASEBALL _____
4. Sheila Burnford _____
5. BICYCLES _____
6. The Borrowers _____
7. Carolyn Sherwin Bailey _____
8. BUTTERFLIES _____
9. Carol Ryrie Brink _____
10. Peter Boston _____

11. Bambi _____
12. BRIDGES _____
13. Virginia Burton _____
14. BASKETBALL _____
15. Judy Blume _____
16. The bronze bow _____
17. The biggest bear _____
18. BIRTHSTONES _____
19. Big Red _____
20. BRAZIL _____

CARD CATALOG WORDSEARCH

```
R  C  W  D  P  U  B  L  I  S  H  E  R  E
Y  C  N  R  E  B  M  U  N  L  L  A  C  I
H  T  O  S  L  A  E  E  S  T  P  N  N  L
P  R  N  P  L  H  K  C  I  J  E  S  R  L
A  C  F  H  Y  K  P  T  B  R  I  O  N  U
R  B  I  C  F  R  D  C  E  D  H  T  X  S
G  L  C  H  T  P  I  F  E  T  B  E  H  T
O  U  T  S  I  D  E  G  U  I  D  E  S  R
I  H  I  R  K  R  U  A  H  N  C  U  K  A
B  R  O  C  S  I  J  X  I  T  B  Y  O  T
Y  D  N  S  D  R  A  C  B  J  D  S  O  O
S  P  O  E  D  R  A  W  E  R  S  A  B  R
R  R  S  N  O  I  T  C  I  F  X  E  T  P
C  A  R  D  C  A  T  A  L  O  G  S  E  E
```

DIRECTIONS: Encircle the words listed below. The words may be found forward, backward, diagonally, horizontally or vertically.

Author	Copyright	Illustrator	Rods
Biography	Cross Reference	Index	See
Books	Drawers	Inside Guides	See Also
Call Number	Easy	Nonfiction	Subject
Card Catalog	Fiction	Publisher	Title
Cards			

FEBRUARY

Lesson 1

SKILL: Knowledge and understanding of biography and autobiography.

OBJECTIVE: Students will begin an activity designed to review and reinforce knowledge of biography and autobiography.

LITERATURE: Biography. Newbery biography.

PREPARATION: A copy of "Who Am I?" for each student. A transparency for introduction. Overhead projector. Prepare an introduction to biography. Display biographies. Place folders on tables.

LESSON: Students take assigned seats. Check attendance. Review biography and autobiography. Hand out activity. Using transparency, introduce activity. Students will have until the end of the fourth lesson to complete activity. Introduce biography. Tell briefly of books on display.

BOOK SELECTION: Students return to tables. Review lesson. Dismiss by tables. Collect folders.

Lesson 2

SKILL: Knowledge and understanding of biography and autobiography.

OBJECTIVE: Students will continue activity designed to review and reinforce knowledge of biography and autobiography.

LITERATURE: Biography.

PREPARATION: Lined paper for students. Transparency of activity. Overhead projector. Display biographies. Place folders on tables.

LESSON: Students take assigned seats. Check attendance. Using transparency, review activity. Have students continue activity. Tell briefly of books on display.

BOOK SELECTION: Students return to tables. Review and discuss progress of activity. Dismiss by tables. Collect folders.

Lesson 3

SKILL: Knowledge and understanding of biography and autobiography.

OBJECTIVE: Students will continue activity designed to review and reinforce knowledge of biography and autobiography.

LITERATURE: Biography.

PREPARATION: Lined paper for students. Transparency of activity. Overhead projector. Display biographies. Place folders on tables.

LESSON: Students take assigned seats. Check attendance. Using transparency, review progress of activity. Have students continue activity. Tell briefly of books on display.

BOOK SELECTION: Students return to tables. Review lesson. Remind students that the activity must be finished next lesson. Dismiss by tables. Collect folders.

Lesson 4

SKILL: Knowledge and understanding of biography and autobiography.

OBJECTIVE: Students will complete an activity designed to review and reinforce knowledge and understanding of biography and autobiography.

LITERATURE: Biography.

PREPARATION: Lined paper for students. Transparency of activity. Overhead projector. Display biographies. Place folders on tables.

LESSON: Students take assigned seats. Check attendance. Using transparency, review progress of activity. Students must complete activity during this lesson. The reports will be displayed in the library or classrooms without the name of the student or person. Students will try to guess "Who Am I?" Tell briefly of books on display.

BOOK SELECTION: Students return to tables. Discuss results of the activity. Dismiss by tables. Collect folders.

Name _____   Date _____

WHO AM I?

© 1988 by The Center for Applied Research in Education

DIRECTIONS: Choose a famous person. Research this person using encyclopedias, biographical dictionaries, and books. Use this outline as a guide.

Then, pretending to be this person, write an autobiography. Remember to give all important facts, accomplishments, and credits. The autobiographies will be displayed for the class to guess *WHO AM I?* Do not write your name or the name of the person on your report.

OUTLINE GUIDE

   I. Where and when person was born

 II. Childhood

     A. Information about family and pets

     B. Places the person lived

     C. Education

     D. Special events in the person's childhood

III. Adulthood

     A. Career(s)

     B. Credits

     C. Accomplishments

IV. Why person is considered famous

 V. Today

     A. If person is no longer living, give time and place of death

     B. If person is still living, give plans for future

MARCH

Lesson 1

SKILL: Knowledge and understanding of the Dewey Decimal Classification System.

OBJECTIVE: Students will review and reinforce their knowledge of the Dewey Decimal Classification System.

LITERATURE: Science fiction. Newbery Science fiction.

PREPARATION: Several blank transparencies. Overhead projector. Prepare an introduction to science fiction. Display science fiction. Place folders on tables.

LESSON: Students take assigned seats. Check attendance. Introduce, review, and discuss the Dewey Decimal Classification System. Using a blank transparency, write 000 at top. Have students contribute all the subjects they can for that main class. Do one transparency for each main class through 900. Introduce science fiction. Tell briefly of books on display.

BOOK SELECTION: Students return to tables. Review lesson. Dismiss by tables. Collect folders.

Lesson 2

SKILL: Knowledge and understanding of the Dewey Decimal Classification System.

OBJECTIVE: Students will assign main numbers to a list of subjects.

LITERATURE: Science fiction.

PREPARATION: A copy of the activity "What Main Class Am I?" for each student. A transparency of activity for introduction. Overhead projector. Display science fiction. Place folders on tables.

LESSON: Students take assigned seats. Check attendance. Introduce activity. Have students complete activity. Tell briefly of books on display.

BOOK SELECTION: Students return to tables. Review lesson. Dismiss by tables. Collect folders.

Lesson 3

SKILL: Knowledge and understanding of the Dewey Decimal Classification System.

OBJECTIVE: Students will search out subjects with the main classes of Dewey in preparation for a Dewey Decimal Bee.

LITERATURE: Science fiction.

PREPARATION: A copy of "Dewey Decimal Bee" for each student. A transparency for introduction. Overhead projector. Display science fiction. Place folders on tables.

LESSON: Students take assigned seats. Check attendance. Hand out materials. Using transparency, introduce activity. Assign each table a main class to begin with, to avoid confusion and crowding. If you plan to have students cut sheet into strips, have scissors and a box available, or have students turn in sheet for you to choose and cut. Have students complete activity. Tell briefly of books on display.

BOOK SELECTION: Students return to tables. Explain that next week, class will hold a Dewey Decimal Bee. Class will be divided into two teams. Dismiss by tables. Collect folders.

Lesson 4

SKILL: Knowledge and understanding of the Dewey Decimal Classification System.

OBJECTIVE: Students will engage in a Dewey Decimal Bee.

LITERATURE: Science fiction.

PREPARATION: Activity sheet cut into strips, folded, and placed in a box. Large sheet of paper for keeping score, marked A and B. Display science fiction. Place folders on tables.

LESSON: Students take assigned seats. Check attendance. Divide class into two teams, A and B. Try to arrange seating so teams face each other.
1. Draw a slip from the box. Read the title. The first player on team A will give main class. If correct, award point, and draw title for team B. If incorrect, go to first player on team B. Continue for length of time available. Count up score. Team with most points wins.
Tell briefly of books on display.

BOOK SELECTION: Students return to tables. Review unit. Dismiss by tables. Collect folders.

Name _____   Date _____

WHAT MAIN CLASS AM I?

000	100	200	300	400
500	600	700	800	900

DIRECTIONS: Assign a main class number to each of the following titles.

1. George. *The Wild Wild Cook Book.* _____

2. Ardley. *Discovering Electricity.* _____

3. Gibbons. *Tunnels.* _____

4. Laiken. *Listen to Me, I'm Angry.* _____

5. Coombs. *Be a Winner in Soccer.* _____

6. Berger. *The Public Education System.* _____

7. Efron. *Bible Stories You Can't Forget.* _____

8. Morton. *A Harvest of Russian Children's Literature.* _____

9. Guinness. *The Guinness Book of World Records.* _____

10. Rudolph. *You Can Learn Russian.* _____

11. Clayton. *Martin Luther King.* _____

12. Lindop. *The First Book of Elections.* _____

13. Lamb. *Tales from Shakespeare.* _____

14. Zaidenberg. *How to Draw a Circus.* _____

15. Berger. *Sports Medicine.* _____

16. Robson. *My Parents Are Divorced Too.* _____

17. Glubok. *Knights in Armor.* _____

18. Arnold. *The Winter Olympics.* _____

19. Gilfond. *The Northeast States.* _____

DEWEY DECIMAL BEE

DIRECTIONS: Go to the shelf, beginning at the main number that is assigned to your group. Choose one title from each main number. Try to use a different title from anyone else. Write the author, the title, and the call number. Return to your seat. Cut the paper into strips on the solid lines. Fold the strips and deposit them into the box.

Author	Title	Call Number
000		
100		
200		
300		
400		
500		
600		
700		
800		
900		

APRIL

Lesson 1

SKILL: Knowledge and understanding of the almanac.

OBJECTIVE: Students will complete an activity designed to afford practice locating information in the almanac.

LITERATURE: Realistic problem-solving fiction and nonfiction. Newbery realistic fiction.

PREPARATION: A World Almanac for each two students. A copy of "Fun With the Almanac, Part 1" for each student. A transparency of activity. Overhead projector. Prepare an introduction to realistic problem-solving fiction and nonfiction. Display books on the genre. Place folders on tables.

LESSON: Students take assigned seats. Check attendance. Hand out materials. Review and discuss how to use the almanac. Using transparency, introduce activity. Have students complete activity. Complete activity with class on transparency. Introduce genre. Tell briefly of books on display.

BOOK SELECTION: Students return to tables. Review lesson. Dismiss by tables. Collect folders.

Lesson 2

SKILL: Knowledge and understanding of the almanac.

OBJECTIVE: Students will complete an activity designed to afford practice in locating information in the almanac.

LITERATURE: Realistic problem-solving fiction and nonfiction.

PREPARATION: A World Almanac for each two students. A copy of "Fun With the Almanac, Part 2" for each student. A transparency for introduction. Overhead projector. Display books on genre. Place folders on tables.

LESSON: Students take assigned seats. Check attendance. Hand out materials. Using transparency, introduce activity. Have students complete the activity. Complete activity on transparency with class. Tell briefly of books on display.

BOOK SELECTION: Students return to tables. Review lesson. Dismiss by tables. Collect folders.

Lesson 3

SKILL: Knowledge and understanding of the almanac.

OBJECTIVE: Students will devise questions for the whole class to answer using the almanac.

LITERATURE: Realistic problem-solving fiction and nonfiction.

PREPARATION: An almanac for each two students. Lined paper for students. Display books on genre. Place folders on tables.

LESSON: Students take assigned seats. Check attendance. Introduce activity. Students will browse through almanac locating interesting facts. Each two students will devise five questions from the information given in the almanac. Students will write questions and answer them, giving the page number of the answer. Collect questions. Tell briefly of books on display.

BOOK SELECTION: Students return to tables. Review lesson. Dismiss by tables. Collect folders.

Lesson 4

SKILL: Knowledge and understanding of the almanac.

OBJECTIVE: Students will locate information in the almanac to answer questions devised by their peers.

LITERATURE: Realistic problem-solving fiction and nonfiction.

PREPARATION: One almanac for each two students. Go over student questions. Mark each paper 1 to 5, with 1 being the best question. Several blank transparencies. Overhead projector. Display books on genre. Place folders on tables.

LESSON: Students take assigned seats. Check attendance. Have one pair begin. Ask question one. Write on transparency. Class locates answer. The first pair that answers correctly will ask the next question. Continue as long as time allows. Tell briefly of books on display.

BOOK SELECTION: Students return to tables. Review unit. Dismiss by tables. Collect folders.

Name _____   Date _____

FUN WITH THE ALMANAC, PART 1

DIRECTIONS: Using the World Almanac locate the answers to the questions.

1. On what month, day, and year was the Boy Scouts of America founded?
_____

2. What were the four freedoms President Roosevelt termed essential in a speech to Congress on January 6, 1941?
_____   _____

_____   _____

3. Who was the ruler of Rome in 54 AD?
_____

4. On what month, day, and year did the Empire State Building open in New York?
_____

5. What are the odds against a royal flush in poker?
_____

6. On what day, month, and year was Dr. Martin Luther King assassinated?
_____

7. On what day, month, and year was gold discovered in California? How many prospectors came to California the following year?
_____

8. When did the United States drop the gold standard? Give the month, day, and year it was ratified by Congress.
_____

9. What is the road mileage from Boston to San Francisco?
_____

Name _____   Date _____

FUN WITH THE ALMANAC, PART 2

DIRECTIONS: Use the World Almanac to locate the answers to the questions.

1. What document does a citizen need to obtain a passport?

   _____

2. When did the Opium War in China begin and end? What did China cede as a result of this war?

   _____

3. For what discovery did Canadian Frederick G. Banting win a Nobel Prize? In What Year?

   _____

4. Where in the United States is the National Arboretum? When is it open to the public?

   _____

5. On what day, month, and year did the first licensed radio station begin broadcasting?

   _____

6. What is the Roman Numeral for:

   50_____ 100_____ 1,000_____

7. On what day, month, and year was "Old Ironsides" launched in Boston?

   _____

8. What United States magazine had the largest circulation in the year of your almanac? What was the circulation?

   Year _____ Magazine _____ Circulation_____

9. What is the name for the currency in Norway? In Mexico?

   Norway _____ Mexico _____

MAY

Lesson 1

SKILL: Knowledge and understanding of the *Readers' Guide to Periodical Literature* (published by the H. W. Wilson Company).

OBJECTIVE: Students will be introduced to the *Readers' Guide.*

LITERATURE: Humorous fiction and nonfiction. Newbery humorous fiction.

PREPARATION: Semi-monthly, monthly, and annual issues of the *Readers' Guide.* A copy of "The Readers' Guide" for each student. A transparency for introduction. Overhead projector. Prepare an introduction to humorous fiction and nonfiction. Display books in genre. Place folders on tables.

LESSON: Students take assigned seats. Check attendance. Hand out materials. Using transparency, introduce and discuss the Readers' Guide. Have students browse through issues. Introduce humorous fiction and nonfiction. Tell briefly of books on display.

BOOK SELECTION: Students return to tables. Review lesson. Dismiss by tables. Collect folders.

Lesson 2

SKILL: Knowledge and understanding of the *Readers' Guide.*

OBJECTIVE: Students will practice decoding abbreviations used in the *Readers' Guide.*

PREPARATION: An issue of *Readers' Guide* for each two students. A copy of "Abbreviations Used in the Readers' Guide" for each student. A transparency for introduction. Overhead projector. Display humorous fiction and nonfiction. Place folders on tables.

LESSON: Students take assigned seats. Check attendance. Hand out materials. Using transparency, introduce activity. Demonstrate the page on which the abbreviations are located. Have students complete activity. Complete activity with class on transparency. Tell briefly of books on display.

BOOK SELECTION: Students return to tables. Review lesson. Dismiss by tables. Collect folders.

Lesson 3

SKILL: Knowledge and understanding of the *Readers' Guide.*

OBJECTIVE: Students will practice decoding entries in the *Readers' Guide.*

LITERATURE: Humorous fiction and nonfiction.

PREPARATION: A copy of "The Readers' Guide: Decoding an Entry." A transparency for introduction. Overhead projector. Display humorous fiction and nonfiction. Place folders on tables.

LESSON: Students take assigned seats. Check attendance. Hand out materials. Using transparency, introduce activity. Have students complete activity. Complete activity with class on transparency. Tell briefly of books on display.

BOOK SELECTION: Students return to tables. Review lesson. Dismiss by tables. Collect folders.

Lesson 4

SKILL: Knowledge and understanding of the *Readers' Guide.*

OBJECTIVE: Students will prepare a bibliography on a subject, using the Readers' Guide.

LITERATURE: Humorous fiction and nonfiction.

PREPARATION: Issues of *Readers' Guide.* Lined paper. Display a selection of humorous fiction and nonfiction. Place folders on tables.

LESSON: Students take assigned seats. Check attendance. Have students choose a subject. Have students prepare a bibliography, using issues of the *Readers' Guide.* Students will use the bibliographic format used in your district. Tell briefly of books on display.

BOOK SELECTION: Students return to tables. Review unit. Dismiss by tables. Collect folders.

Name _____   Date _____

THE READERS' GUIDE TO PERIODICAL LITERATURE

A great deal of information can be retrieved from magazines. However, trying to locate information from magazines can be time-consuming.

The *Readers' Guide* is an index to articles printed in magazines. Most magazines published are indexed in the *Readers' Guide*. Articles can be located in the *Readers' Guide* by author and subject, as well as cross-references.

The *Readers' Guide* is issued semimonthly. The semimonthly guide contains the past two weeks of indexing of magazine articles. The *Readers' Guide* is published by the H.W. Wilson Company.

A monthly guide is also issued which contains the past four weeks of indexing of magazine articles.

A quarterly guide is issued which contains three months of indexing of magazine articles.

The hardbound volume contains a full year of indexing of magazine articles.

The alphabetical listing of magazines indexed in the *Readers' Guide* is found in the front section of each issue.

Each entry in the *Readers' Guide* is abbreviated. The list of abbreviations for each magazine title is found in the front section of each issue.

Other abbreviations used in each entry are found in a list in the front section of each issue.

Using the *Readers' Guide* is easy after a bit of practice with abbreviations and decoding the entries.

You do not have to spend hours checking each magazine title and issue, hoping to find information on your subject. All you have to do is check your subject or author in the *Readers' Guide,* beginning with the latest issue and working backwards. When you have found the entry, write down the title and issue and request the magazine at the reference desk.

You must know the abbreviations and how to decode the entry in order to understand what magazine and issue to request. The following activity sheets will give you a chance to practice decoding entries.

Name _____   Date _____

ABBREVIATIONS FOUND IN THE READERS' GUIDE TO PERIODICAL LITERATURE

DIRECTIONS: Locate the abbreviation's index for magazine titles in the *Readers' Guide*. Write the full name of the magazine on the blank line.

1. Archit Dig _____

2. Am Hist Illus _____

3. Bull At Sci _____

4. Creat Crafts Miniat _____

5. Un Mon Chron _____

DIRECTIONS: Locate the abbreviation's index in the *Readers' Guide*. Write the meaning of the abbreviation on the blank line.

6. ann _____	16. pub _____
7. bi-m _____	17. q _____
8. bibl _____	18. rev _____
9. cont _____	19. soc _____
10. il _____	20. sp _____
11. no _____	21. tr _____
12. + _____	22. v _____
13. Jl _____	23. yr _____
14. Ag _____	24. Mr _____
15. O _____	25. Je _____

Name _____   Date _____

THE READERS' GUIDE: DECODING AN ENTRY

> AUTHORSHIP
> If you want to write poetry for children.
> M.C. Livingston. Writer 98: 24 − 6 + AG
> '85

SUBJECT: AUTHORSHIP
AUTHOR: M.C. LIVINGSTON
TITLE OF ARTICLE: If you want to write
poetry for children
MAGAZINE TITLE: Writer

VOLUME NUMBER: 98
PAGES: 24 through 26
+: Continued on later pages in the same issue
MONTH: August
YEAR: 1985

DIRECTIONS: Decode the following entries.

1.

> CHILDREN—GROWTH AND DEVELOPMENT
> Kids teach each other kindness. [Research by
> Nancy Eisenberg] E. Stark. Psychol Today
> 19: 11 + Ag '85

SUBJECT _____   VOLUME NUMBER _____
AUTHOR _____   PAGES _____
TITLE OF ARTICLE _____   MONTH _____
_____   YEAR _____
MAGAZINE TITLE _____

2.

> Hokanson, Drake
> To cross America, early motorists took a long
> detour. i1 Smithsonian 16: 58-65 Ag '85

AUTHOR _____   VOLUME NUMBER _____
TITLE OF ARTICLE _____   PAGES _____
_____   MONTH _____
_____   YEAR _____
MAGAZINE TITLE _____   ILLUSTRATIONS? _____

JUNE

Lesson 1

SKILL: Practice using reference tools.

OBJECTIVE: Students will begin a project designed to afford practice using various reference tools.

LITERATURE: Fiction and nonfiction with foreign setting. Newbery books with foreign setting.

PREPARATION: A copy of the activity "A Grand Tour" for each student. A transparency for introduction. Overhead projector. Reference tools. Prepare an introduction to fiction and nonfiction with foreign setting. Display books on the genre. Place folders on tables.

LESSON: Students take assigned seats. Check attendance. Hand out activity. Using transparency introduce activity. Students will have four class lessons to work on project. Introduce genre. Tell briefly of books on display.

BOOK SELECTION: Students return to tables. Review project. Dismiss by tables. Collect folders.

Lesson 2

SKILL: Practice with reference tools.

OBJECTIVE: Students will continue project designed to afford practice using various reference tools.

LITERATURE: Fiction and nonfiction with foreign setting.

PREPARATION: Transparency of activity. Overhead projector. Lined paper for students. Reference tools. Display genre. Place folders on tables.

LESSON: Students take assigned seats. Check attendance. Have students continue project. Tell briefly of books on display.

BOOK SELECTION: Students return to tables. Review progress of project. Dismiss by tables. Collect folders.

Lesson 3

SKILL: Practice using reference tools.

OBJECTIVE: Students will continue project designed to afford practice using various reference tools.

LITERATURE: Fiction and nonfiction with foreign setting.

PREPARATION: Transparency of activity. Overhead projector. Lined paper for students. Reference tools. Display genre. Place folders on tables.

LESSON: Students take assigned seats. Check attendance. Using transparency review project. Have students continue project. Tell briefly of books on display.

BOOK SELECTION: Students return to tables. Review progress of project. Project must be completed next lesson. Dismiss by tables. Collect folders.

Lesson 4

SKILL: Practice using reference tools.

OBJECTIVE: Students will complete project designed to afford practice in using reference tools.

LITERATURE: As this is the last lesson, there will be no book selection.

PREPARATION: Transparency of activity. Overhead projector. Lined paper. Place folders on tables.

LESSON: Students take assigned seats. Check attendance. Using transparency, review project. Have students complete project. Collect to grade. This project makes an interesting bulletin board for the classroom. Discuss any summer reading programs available. Folders go home with the students. Dismiss by tables.

Name _____   Date _____

A GRAND TOUR

DIRECTIONS: You are going to plan a month-long expense-paid trip to any country, outside your own country.

I. General preparations.

   A. Choose the country. Explain your choice.
   B. Choose the month you will go.
   C. You will depart from the capital of your state and arrive in the capital of the country you are visiting.

II. Specific preparations.

   A. You must obtain a passport. Explain the process.
   B. What is the language of the country? How will you prepare for the language.
   C. You must exchange your money for the currency of the country. What is the currency called? How much or many equal one dollar?
   D. Research the climate of the country for the month you will be there. What type of clothing will you pack?

III. Travel

   A. How will you travel to the country? Approximately how many miles is it to the country? About how long will it take you to get there?

IV. The visit

   A. What city or cities will you visit?
   B. How will you travel about? What modes of transportation are available?
   C. What places will you visit? Be specific.
   D. How will you communicate with the people?
   E. What type of food will you be expected to eat?
   F. What will you purchase as souvenirs or gifts?

V. Travel home

   A. How will you travel home? What will be your departure and arrival points?

VI. Value of the trip

   A. What do you feel you would gain from such a trip?

GRADE 6

OVERVIEW

By sixth grade, students should be proficient in information location, retrieval, and interpretation skills. If classes are scheduled, the activities should be closely correlated to the classroom curriculum. Classwork in the library should consist of individual and small group activities and projects to review and reinforce skills. Monthly genres will be introduced to assist students to continue to develop individual tastes and interests in literature.

Skills

Regulations and procedures	Newspapers
Parts of the book	Indexes
Concepts and parts of the story	Guides to quotations
Book reports	Card catalog
Taking notes	Biography
Outlining	Dewey Decimal System
Paraphrasing	Library of Congress Classification
Bibliography	Elements of fiction
Readers' Guide	Reference sources

Literature

Family—school	Science fiction
Mystery—detective	Realistic problem solving
Historical	Adventure—sports
Fantasy	Humorous
Biography	Foreign setting

SEPTEMBER

Lesson 1

SKILL: Knowledge of the procedures and resources of the library.

OBJECTIVE: Students will review the procedures and resources of the library.

LITERATURE: Family and school fiction and nonfiction.

PREPARATION: A copy of "The Library." Laminate, cut into strips. Prepare an introduction to genre. Display genre. Class roster.

LESSON: Students sit where they wish. Permanent seating will be assigned next week. Check attendance. Activity may be accomplished in two ways.

1. Pass out one slip to each two students. After a length of time, students report question and answer to class.
2. Pass out slips. Students ask the questions of the librarian who answers the questions and leads discussion.

Introduce family and school fiction and nonfiction. Tell briefly of books on display.

BOOK SELECTION: Students return to tables. Beginning next week, students will record books read at beginning of class. Students will be required to read one book per month. The fourth lesson each month will revolve around the book read by each student. Dismiss by tables.

Lesson 2

SKILL: Knowledge of the parts of the book.

OBJECTIVE: Students will complete an activity on the parts of the book.

LITERATURE: Family and school fiction and nonfiction.

PREPARATION: A copy of "Parts of the Book Word Search" for each student. A transparency for introduction. Overhead projector. Materials for folders. A copy of reading record (fourth grade September). Display genre. Permanent seating plan.

LESSON: Assign permanent seating. Check attendance while students record books read. Introduce activity on transparency. Have students complete activity. Complete together on transparency. Tell briefly of books on display.

BOOK SELECTION: Students return to tables. Remind students they must have a fiction book read by the fourth lesson. Have students place folders in middle of table. Dismiss by tables. Collect folders.

Lesson 3

SKILL: Knowledge of the concepts and parts of the story.

OBJECTIVE: Students will complete an activity on the concepts and parts of the story.

LITERATURE: Family and school fiction and nonfiction.

PREPARATION: A copy of "Parts of the Story Word Search" for each student. A transparency for introduction. Display genre. Place folders on tables.

LESSON: Students take assigned seats. Check attendance. Using transparency, introduce activity. Have students complete activity. Complete together with class on transparency. Tell briefly of books on display.

BOOK SELECTION: Students return to tables. Remind students they must have a fiction book read and *in hand* for next week's lesson. Dismiss by tables. Collect folders.

Lesson 4

SKILL: Knowledge and understanding of the preparation of a book report.

OBJECTIVE: Students will practice preparing for a book report.

LITERATURE: Family and school fiction and nonfiction.

PREPARATION: This activity is most successful when coordinated with classroom activity. Plan with the teacher to have a book report due the week following the fourth lesson of each month. A copy of "Book Facts and Opinions" for each student. (This form will be used for each fourth lesson of the month.) A transparency for introduction. Overhead projector. Display genre. Place folders on tables.

LESSON: Students take assigned seats. Check attendance. Students must have book read and in hand. Hand out activity. Using transparency, introduce and complete activity with students. Students will take activity sheet with them to write book report. Tell briefly of books on display.

BOOK SELECTION: Students return to seats. Review lesson. Dismiss by tables. Collect folders.

THE LIBRARY

1. Where's the fiction section?

2. Where's the nonfiction section?

3. Where are the magazines? May I check out magazines?

4. Where are the biography books?

5. Where are the records and tapes? May I check out records and tapes?

6. Where are the encyclopedias? What titles are available?

7. Where are the atlases?

8. Where are the dictionaries?

9. Where are the almanacs?

10. Where are the author reference books? What titles are available?

11. Where are the biographical dictionaries?

12. What's a gazetteer? Where is it?

13. What other kinds of reference books are available?

14. Where are the newspapers? Can I come in every morning and read the paper?

15. Where's the vertical file?

Name _____   Date _____

PARTS OF THE BOOK WORDSEARCH

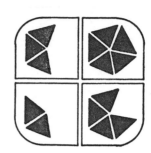

DIRECTIONS: Locate and encircle the *fourteen* parts of the book hidden in the puzzle. The words may be found forwards, backwards, up, down, or diagonally. Write the terms on the lines below as you find them.

```
P D T R T W B S Y L W A H N S
T P E C J G X L H N B P S T H
D G K D T F V Z P L H P N G F
R N C J I H S B A J C E H N R
B P A K T C B E R H T N K Z O
S X J T L M A H G N J D C D N
R N T M E J T T O A X I H X T
C R S G P N P C I M P X E C I
O S U J A C F M L O K D T R S
V N D W G O K N B T N R W B P
E C A F E R P D I I G P L K I
R X C L N J B C B F T S A H E
T R B J I Z Y R A S S O L G C
H A H B P D G L N V D P C F E
T V E R S O P A G E L T S B G
```

1. _____   8. _____

2. _____   9. _____

3. _____   10. _____

4. _____   11. _____

5. _____   12. _____

6. _____   13. _____

7. _____   14. _____

PARTS OF THE STORY WORDSEARCH

DIRECTIONS: Locate and encircle the *fourteen* parts of the story hidden in the puzzle. The words may be found forwards, backwards, up, down, or diagonally. Write the terms on the lines below as you find them.

```
E G P T S V W R H L N D H
F T R O T A R T S U L L I
E C A J B C N I M K G S D
U M C D F D L T E R N E G
G N I T T E S L T R S S H
O N J O C H B E E C R S C
L D A L J B G M R M C R N
A T U P U B L I S H E R O
I D T G N H P J R C F H I
D C H A P T E R S Y D R T
T P O H I K C P C N P M C
S C R O C F T D F S H O A
B L N S R E T D A R A H C
```

1. _____   8. _____

2. _____   9. _____

3. _____   10. _____

4. _____   11. _____

5. _____   12. _____

6. _____   13. _____

7. _____   14. _____

Name _____   Date _____

BOOK FACTS AND OPINIONS
(Page 1)

FACTS:

AUTHOR _____

TITLE _____

PUBLISHER _____

COPYRIGHT DATE _____ NUMBER OF PAGES _____

AWARDS _____ DATE _____

SEQUELS OR PREQUELS _____

GENRE _____ SETTING _____

CHARACTERS: MAIN _____

SUPPORTING _____

PROBLEM _____

_____

_____

PLOT: BEGINNING _____

_____

_____

_____

MIDDLE _____

_____

_____

END _____

_____

_____

BOOK FACTS AND OPINIONS
(Page 2)

OPINIONS:

CHARACTERS

List name and
opinion of
important
characters

_____
_____
_____
_____
_____

DESCRIPTION

Not enough
Enough ➡ Why
Too Much

_____
_____
_____
_____

ACTION

Not enough
Enough ➡ Why
Too Much

_____
_____
_____
_____

DIALOGUE

Not enough
Enough ➡ Why
Too Much

_____
_____
_____
_____

AUTHOR'S STYLE

Liked/disliked
because

_____
_____
_____

CHANGE IN MAIN
CHARACTER FROM
BEGINNING TO END

_____
_____

AUTHOR'S MESSAGE
OR THEME OF THE BOOK

_____
_____

OCTOBER

Lesson 1

SKILL: Knowledge and understanding of *Roget's Thesaurus of English Words and Phrases*. New York: St. Martin's Press.

OBJECTIVE: Students will be introduced to Roget's.

LITERATURE: Mystery and detective fiction and nonfiction.

PREPARATION: Copies of Roget's *Thesaurus*. A copy of activity "Roget's Thesaurus of English Words and Phrases" for each student. A transparency for introduction. Overhead projector. Prepare an introduction to genre. Display genre. Place folders on tables.

LESSON: Students take assigned seats. Check attendance. Hand out materials. Using transparency, have students practice using a thesaurus. Introduce genre. Tell briefly of books on display.

BOOK SELECTION: Students return to tables. Review lesson. Dismiss by tables. Collect folders.

Lesson 2

SKILL: Knowledge and understanding of Roget's *Thesaurus*.

OBJECTIVE: Students will have practice using Roget's.

LITERATURE: Mystery and detective fiction and nonfiction.

PREPARATION: Copies of Roget's *Thesaurus*. A copy of "Practice With Roget's" for each student. A transparency for introduction. Overhead projector. Display genre. Place folders on tables.

LESSON: Students take assigned seats. Check attendance. Using transparency, review Roget's. Hand out materials. Using transparency, introduce activity. Have students complete activity. Complete activity with class on transparency. Tell briefly of books on display.

BOOK SELECTION: Students return to tables. Review lesson. Dismiss by tables. Collect folders.

Lesson 3

SKILL: Knowledge and understanding of Bartlett's Familiar Quotations. Bartlett, John. *Familiar Quotations A Collection of Passages, Phrases and Proverbs*

Traced to their Source in Ancient and Modern Literature. Boston: Little, Brown and Company, 1980.

LITERATURE: Mystery and detective fiction and nonfiction.

PREPARATION: Copies of Bartlett's. A copy of both "Familiar Quotations" and "Practice With Bartlett's" for each student. Transparencies for introduction. Overhead projector. Display genre. Place folders on tables.

LESSON: Students take assigned seats. Check attendance. Using transparency, introduce Bartlett's. Hand out materials. Using transparency, introduce activity. Complete activity with class. Tell briefly of books on display.

BOOK SELECTION: Students return to tables. Review lesson. Dismiss by tables. Collect folders.

Lesson 4

SKILL: Knowledge and understanding of book report preparation.

OBJECTIVE: Students will prepare for a book report.

LITERATURE: Mystery and detective fiction and nonfiction.

PREPARATION: A copy of September's "Book Facts and Opinions" for each student. A transparency for introduction. Overhead projector. Display genre. Place folders on tables.

LESSON: Students take assigned seats. Check attendance. Students are to have books read and in hand. Hand out materials. Using transparency, complete activity with the class. Activity goes with students to prepare a book report for the classroom teacher. Tell briefly of books on display.

BOOK SELECTION: Students return to tables. Review lesson. Dismiss by tables. Collect folders.

ROGET'S THESAURUS OF ENGLISH WORDS AND PHRASES

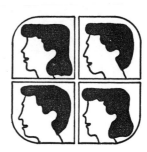

Roget's Thesaurus is a book of synonyms and antonyms. It is divided into main classes and divisions. When first using Roget's, leaf through it. Each entry has a number. The number of entries included on a page are printed at the top of each page, similar to guide words, but in this case guide numbers.

Each entry gives synonyms of the word used as a noun, adjective, verb, and adverb, plus a "See" reference to other entries.

To use *Roget's Thesaurus,* locate the word you wish to replace in the alphabetically arranged index. Check the subheadings listed under the word and follow the reference given.

DIRECTIONS FOR PRACTICE:

1. Locate the word *SEVERE* in the index.

   a. How many synonyms are listed? _____.

   b. How many are nouns? _____.

   c. How many are verbs? _____.

   d. How many are adjectives? _____.

   e. How many are adverbs? _____.

   f. If you wanted a synonym for *SEVERE* that is an antonym of *LIGHTHEARTED,* which synonym would you choose?

   _____

   g. If you wanted a synonym for *SEVERE* that is an antonym of *FANCY,* which one would you choose?

   _____

2. Think of several words and check those words in the index. Find a synonym for those words.

PRACTICE WITH ROGET'S

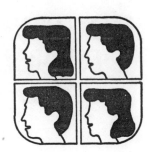

DIRECTIONS: Complete the following.

1. Look up the word *BLINK*. Which synonym would fit best in this sentence?

   The warning light *blinked* on and off.

   Synonym _____.

   Rewrite the sentence using the synonym.

   _____.

2. Look up the word *INJURY*. Which synonym would fit best in this sentence?

   He was *injured* in battle.

   Synonym _____.

   Rewrite the sentence using the synonym.

   _____.

3. Look up the word *LAUGHTER*. Which synonym would fit best in this sentence?

   "You're too skinny to play football," she *laughed*

   Synonym _____.

   Rewrite the sentence using the synonym.

   _____.

FAMILIAR QUOTATIONS

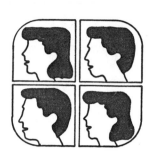

Bartlett's Familiar Quotations is a collection of passages, phrases, and proverbs traced to their source. It is arranged chronologically by the birth years of the authors.

The index to authors is found in the front of the book.

The index to the first line or phrase is found in the back of the book.

The pages in the middle section are divided in half vertically with the left section designated as "a" and the right section designated as "b".

The italics at the end of the entry refer to the source of the work.

IBID. comes from the word Ibidem—meaning in the same place. If the source is the same as the entry above, IBID. is used. If the primary source is the same, but comes from a different part of the work, the difference is added after IBID.

USING BARTLETT'S. Perhaps you know a famous quotation or phrase, but you do not know the author or source. Locate the beginning line or phrase in the index and you will be able to locate the author and the rest of the work.

EXAMPLE: There is a famous inscription on the Statue of Liberty. You cannot remember the whole inscription or the author, but you do know it starts with:…"Give me your tired…".

In the index, you locate, "Give me your tired masses."

You locate the page indicated and find the entire inscription for the Statue of Liberty, written by Emma Lazarus:

"Give me your tired, your poor,
Your huddled masses yearning to
    breathe free,
The wretched refuse of your teeming
    shore,
Send these, the homeless, tempest-
    tossed, to me:
I lift my lamp beside the golden door."

Name _____ Date _____

PRACTICE
WITH BARTLETT'S

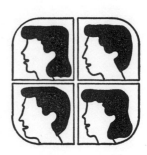

DIRECTIONS: Answer the following questions using the method shown on the information sheet.*

1. Who wrote the work beginning: "One if by land, and two if by sea…"?

   Page _____ Author _____

   Title of work_____

   Title of book_____

2. Who wrote: "All animals are equal, but some animals are more equal than
   others."?

   Page _____ Author _____

   Title of book_____

3. Who wrote: "Always do right. This will gratify some people, and astonish the
   rest."?

   Page _____ Author _____

   Where, when, and to whom?_____

   _____

4. Who wrote: "…for a whaleship was my Yale College and my Harvard."?

   Page _____ Author _____

   Title of book_____

*If the quotation is not listed using the first key word, look for a second or third key
word.

NOVEMBER

Lesson 1

SKILL: Independent location and interpretation of information.

OBJECTIVE: Students will begin a research project that will continue throughout the year. Practice using encyclopedias and almanacs.

LITERATURE: Historical fiction and nonfiction.

PREPARATION: Almanacs and encyclopedias. A copy of "Research Project" for each student. A transparency for introduction. Overhead projector. Prepare an introduction to genre. Display books in genre. Place folders on tables.

LESSON: Students take assigned seats. Check attendance. Hand out activity. Using transparency, introduce activity. Students will have three lessons to complete project. Introduce genre. Tell briefly of books on display.

BOOK SELECTION: Students return to tables. Review lesson. Remind students: a work of historical fiction must be read by the fourth lesson. Dismiss by tables. Collect folders.

Lesson 2

SKILL: Independent location and interpretation of information.

OBJECTIVE: Students will continue project.

LITERATURE: Historical fiction and nonfiction.

PREPARATION: Almanacs and encyclopedias. Transparency of project. Overhead projector. Lined paper. Display books in genre. Place folders on tables.

LESSON: Students take assigned seats. Check attendance. Using transparency, review project. Have students continue project. Tell briefly of books on display.

BOOK SELECTION: Students return to tables. Review progress of project. Dismiss by tables. Collect folders.

Lesson 3

SKILL: Independent location and interpretation of information.

OBJECTIVE: Students will complete project.

LITERATURE: Historical fiction and nonfiction.

PREPARATION: Almanacs and encyclopedias. Transparency of project. Overhead projector. Lined paper. Display books in genre. Place folders on tables.

LESSON: Students take assigned seats. Check attendance. Using transparency, review project. Students will complete project. Tell briefly of books on display.

BOOK SELECTION: Students return to tables. Review project. Remind students they must have a work of historical fiction read and in hand for next week's lesson.

Lesson 4

SKILL: Knowledge and understanding of book report preparation.

OBJECTIVE: Students will prepare for a book report.

LITERATURE: Historical fiction and nonfiction.

PREPARATION: Copy of "Book Facts and Opinions" for each student. A transparency for introduction. Overhead projector. Display books in genre. Place folders on tables.

LESSON: Students take assigned seats. Check attendance. Students must have a work of historical fiction read and in hand. Hand out activity. Using transparency, complete activity with class. Activity will go with students to prepare for a book report for class. Tell briefly of books on display.

BOOK SELECTION: Students return to tables. Review lesson. Dismiss by tables. Collect folders.

Name _____ Date _____

RESEARCH PROJECT

DIRECTIONS: Select a country other than your own. Select one that truly interests you, as this project will continue in various forms throughout the year. Through the use of almanacs and encyclopedias, locate the information requested below. Record all reference sources used on the back of this sheet, including author, title, place of publication, publisher, and copyright date. You will prepare a bibliography from this information at the end of the year.

1. Name of country _____

2. Statistics

    Capital _____ Area _____

    Population _____ Currency _____

3. History

    Earliest settlements _____

    _____

    Name several important events in history _____

    _____

    _____

    _____

4. Government. What is the present form of government?

    _____

5. Education. What is the average length of schooling?

    _____

DECEMBER

Lesson 1

SKILL: Knowledge and understanding of the Dewey Decimal Classification System.

OBJECTIVE: Students will review and reinforce their knowledge of the Dewey Decimal Classification System.

LITERATURE: Fantasy and/or seasonal fiction and nonfiction.

PREPARATION: Blank transparencies. Overhead projector. Prepare an introduction to genres. Display books in genres. Place folders on tables.

LESSON: Students take assigned seats. Check attendance. Using transparencies, have students give subjects that fall in each main class. Introduce genres. Tell briefly of books on display.

BOOK SELECTION: Students return to tables. Review lesson. Dismiss by tables. Collect folders.

Lesson 2

SKILL: Knowledge and understanding of the Dewey Decimal System.

OBJECTIVE: Students will complete an activity designed to afford practice with individual numbers.

LITERATURE: Fantasy and/or seasonal literature.

PREPARATION: A copy of "Dewey Numbers and Subjects for Activities" and "The Festival Called Christmas" for each student. A transparency for introduction. Overhead projector. Display books in genres. Place folders on tables.

LESSON: Students take assigned seats. Check attendance. Hand out materials. Using transparency, introduce activity. Have students complete activity. Complete activity with class using transparency. Tell briefly of books on display.

BOOK SELECTION: Students return to tables. Review Dewey. Dismiss by tables. Collect folders.

Lesson 3

SKILL: Knowledge and understanding of the Dewey Decimal System.

OBJECTIVE: Students will complete an activity designed to afford practice with individual subject numbers.

LITERATURE: Fantasy and/or seasonal fiction and nonfiction.

PREPARATION: A copy of "The Festival Called Hanukkah" for each student. A transparency for introduction. Display books in genres. Place folders on tables.

LESSON: Students take assigned seats. Check attendance. Hand out activity. Using transparency, introduce activity. Have students complete activity. Complete together with class on transparency. Tell briefly of books on display.

BOOK SELECTION: Students return to tables. Review lesson. Dismiss by tables. Collect folders.

Lesson 4

SKILL: Knowledge and understanding of book report preparation.

OBJECTIVE: Students will practice preparing for a book report.

LITERATURE: Fantasy and/or seasonal fiction and nonfiction.

PREPARATION: A copy of September's "Book Facts and Opinions" for each student. Transparency for introduction. Overhead projector. Display books in genres. Place folders on tables.

LESSON: Students take assigned seats. Check attendance. Hand out activity. Using transparency, complete activity with students. Activity goes with students to classroom to aid in writing the book report. Tell briefly of books on display.

BOOK SELECTION: Students return to tables. Review lesson. Dismiss by tables. Collect folders.

Name _____ Date _____

DEWEY NUMBERS AND SUBJECTS FOR ACTIVITIES

ARMY	355.3	JUDEA	933
BRITISH ISLES	942	LEGEND	398.2
CANDY	641.5	LIGHT	535
CHRIST	232	MARY	232.91
CHRISTIAN	201	MEXICO	972
CHRISTIANITY	201	OIL	553
CHRISTMAS	394.2	RELIGION	200
DAY	529	ROMAN EMPIRE	937
EUROPE	940	SCANDINAVIA	948
FREEDOM OF WORSHIP	323.44	SEASONS	525
GOD	296.3	SPANISH	460
GREECE	938	TELEVISION	621.388
HANUKKAH	296.4	TEMPLE	726
IRELAND	941.5	WORLD	341.2
JOSEPH	232.9		
JUDAISM	296		

Name _____   Date _____

THE FESTIVAL CALLED CHRISTMAS

DIRECTIONS: On the blank line write the subject for the number in parenthesis represented by a Dewey number.
REMEMBER: This is a puzzle activity. You may need to use a different form of the word to best make sense.

In the late 300s (201) _____ became the official (200) _____
                              (1)   (2)
of the (937) _____. By A.D. 1100 (394.2) _____ had become the
                    (3)   (4)
most important religious festival in (940) _____, with St. Nicholas a
                                                    (5)
symbol of gift giving in most of the (940) _____ countries. (394.2)
                                                    (6)
_____ is the celebration of the birth of (232) _____.
        (7)   (8)
Today, (394.2) _____ is celebrated in many ways throughout the world.
                      (9)
In the (942) _____, the children hang up their stockings to be filled
                    (10)
by Father (394.2) _____. On (394.2) _____ Day afternoon, the
                          (11)   (12)
queen speaks to the people on (621.388) _____. In (941.5) _____
                                                (13)   (14)
people put a lighted candle in a window as a sign of welcome to passing
travelers. (394.2) _____ dinner in the (948) _____ countries
                          (15)   (16)
includes a rice pudding containing a single almond. The person finding the
almond in his or her serving is assured of good luck for a year. In (972) _____
                                                                                    (17)
and other (460) _____ speaking countries, the nine (529) _____
                      (18)   (19)
before (394.2) _____ are special. On these (520) _____,
                      (20)   (21)
called posadas, the people reenact the search of (232.91) _____ and (232.9)
                                                                  (22)
_____ to find lodgings on the eve of the birth of (232) _____.
          (23)   (24)
After each posada ceremony, a piñata, a clay or paper figure containing (641.5)
_____ and gifts, is broken and shared. For (201) _____
          (25)   (26)
people everywhere, (394.2) _____ is a (525) _____ of sharing and joy.
                                  (27)   (28)

Name _____   Date _____

THE FESTIVAL CALLED HANUKKAH

DIRECTIONS: On the blank line write the subject for the number in parenthesis represented by a Dewey number.

REMEMBER: This is a puzzle activity. You may need to use a different form of the word to best make sense.

(296.4) _____ is the (296) _____ Feast of (535) _____.
                (1)   (2)   (3)

(296.4) _____ celebrates two important events in the history of (296)
                (4)

_____, the victory of the (296) _____ over King Antiochus
        (5)   (6)

and his Syrian (355.3) _____ and the rededication of the (726)
                              (7)

_____ in Jerusalem to the worship of (296.3) _____
        (8)   (9)

Antiochus Epiphanes, King of Syria, ordered all people in (933) _____
                                                                          (10)

to practice the (938) _____ pagan (200) _____. The (296)
                          (11)   (12)

_____ refused and rebelled. Clearly outnumbered, Judah Maccabee,
        (13)

leading a poorly equipped (355.3) _____ defeated the Syrian (355.3)
                                          (14)

_____ and recaptured Jerusalem. The holy (726) _____ was
        (15)   (16)

rededicated with feasting and joy. According to (398.2) _____, there
                                                                (17)

was only enough (553) _____ to last for one day of (535) _____.
                          (18)   (19)

But the (553) _____ lasted for eight days. The menorah recalls the
                  (20)

miracle of (535) _____. One candle is lit each evening until all are
                      (21)

lit. The celebration gives thanks to (296.3) _____ for the victory
                                                      (22)

that allowed people to have (323.44) _____.
                                              (23)

JANUARY

Lesson 1

SKILL: Knowledge and understanding of the card catalog.

OBJECTIVE: Students will have an overall review of the card catalog.

LITERATURE: Animal fiction and nonfiction.

PREPARATION: Make a transparency of a set of catalog cards. Overhead projector. Some type of media for card catalog review. Prepare an introduction to genre. Display books in genre. Place folders on tables.

LESSON: Students take assigned seats. Check attendance. Using media, review the card catalog. Using transparency, review the three types of catalog cards and the information found on a catalog card. Emphasize the location of the information on the card. Introduce genre. Tell briefly of books on display.

BOOK SELECTION: Students return to tables. Review lesson. Remind students: a work of animal fiction must be read by fourth lesson. Dismiss by tables. Collect folders.

Lesson 2

SKILL: Knowledge and understanding of the card catalog.

OBJECTIVE: Students will design a set of catalog cards for a fiction book.

LITERATURE: Animal fiction and nonfiction.

PREPARATION: A copy of "A Set of Catalog Cards" for each student. A transparency for introduction. The transparency of a set of catalog cards. Overhead projector. Display genre. Place folders on tables.

LESSON: Students take assigned seats. Check attendance. Hand out activity sheets Using transparency, review the location of information found on catalog cards. Students will design a set of catalog cards for a fiction book of their choice, from the book itself. Students will check the author card in the card catalog on completion to compare the results. Tell briefly of books on display.

BOOK SELECTION: Students return to tables. Review lesson. Dismiss by tables. Collect folders.

Lesson 3

SKILL: Knowledge and understanding of the card catalog.

OBJECTIVE: Students will design a set of catalog cards for a nonfiction book.

LITERATURE: Animal fiction and nonfiction.

PREPARATION: A copy of "A Set of Catalog Cards" for each student. Transparency of the blank set and transparency of a set of catalog cards. Overhead projector. Display books in genre. Place folders on tables.

LESSON: Students take assigned seats. Check attendance. Using transparency, review location of information. Hand out materials. Have students design a set of catalog cards for a nonfiction book of their choice, from the book itself. Students will check author card in the card catalog on completion to check results. Tell briefly of books on display.

BOOK SELECTION: Students return to tables. Review lesson. Remind students they must have a work of animal fiction read and in hand next week. Dismiss by tables. Collect folders.

Lesson 4

SKILL: Knowledge and understanding of book report preparation.

OBJECTIVE: Students will practice preparing for a book report.

LITERATURE: Animal fiction and nonfiction.

PREPARATION: A copy of September's "Book Facts and Opinions" for each student. Transparency for introduction. Overhead projector. Display books in genre. Place folders on tables.

LESSON: Students take assigned seats. Check attendance. Hand out activity. Using transparency, complete activity with class. Tell briefly of books on display.

BOOK SELECTION: Students return to tables. Review lesson. Dismiss by tables. Collect folders.

Name _____   Date _____

A SET OF CATALOG CARDS

AUTHOR

TITLE

SUBJECT

FEBRUARY

Lesson 1

SKILL: Practice retrieving biographical information.

OBJECTIVE: Students will locate information concerning famous persons from the country selected for November's project.

LITERATURE: Biography.

PREPARATION: A copy of "Famous Persons from _____" for each student. A transparency for introduction. Overhead projector. Prepare an introduction to biography. Place folders on tables.

LESSON: Students take assigned seats. Check attendance. Hand out activity sheets. Using transparency, introduce activity. Students will have three lessons to complete project. Introduce biography. Tell briefly of books on display.

BOOK SELECTION: Students return to tables. Review lesson. Dismiss by tables. Collect folders.

Lesson 2

SKILL: Practice retrieving biographical information.

OBJECTIVE: Students will continue project started last week.

LITERATURE: Biography.

PREPARATION: Transparency of activity. Overhead projector. Display a selection of biographies. Place folders on tables.

LESSON: Students take assigned seats. Check attendance. Using transparency, review project. Have students continue project. Tell briefly of books on display.

BOOK SELECTION: Students return to tables. Remind students: a biography must be read and in hand for fourth lesson. Review lesson. Dismiss by tables. Collect folders.

Lesson 3

SKILL: Practice retrieving biographical information.

OBJECTIVE: Students will complete project concerned with locating information on famous persons connected with country selected for November's project.

LITERATURE: Biography.

PREPARATION: Transparency of project. Overhead projector. Display selection of biographies. Place folders on tables.

LESSON: Students take assigned seats. Check attendance. Using transparency, review project. Students are to complete project. Tell briefly of books on display.

BOOK SELECTION: Students return to tables. Remind students: a biography must be read and in hand for next week's lesson. Review project. Dismiss by tables. Collect folders.

Lesson 4

SKILL: Knowledge and understanding of book report preparation.

OBJECTIVE: Students will practice preparing for a book report.

LITERATURE: Biography.

PREPARATION: A copy of "Book Facts and Opinions" for each student. A transparency for introduction. Display biography. Place folders on tables.

LESSON: Students take assigned seats. Check attendance. Students must have biography read and in hand. Using transparency, complete the book report form with class, helping and discussing where necessary. Tell briefly of books on display.

BOOK SELECTION: Students return to tables. Book report sheets go with students to classroom to help in writing their book reports. Dismiss by tables. Collect folders

---

Name _____   Date _____

FAMOUS PERSONS
FROM _____

DIRECTIONS: Using the country you chose for November's project, find the **names of** *5* important or well-known people from that country.

If you have difficulty locating the names of *5* people, check the following sources:

1. Biographical dictionaries—index.
2. Card catalog—subject heading BIOGRAPHY following the subject heading for your country.
3. World Book Encyclopedia—"Related Articles" section at the end of the article of your country.
4. Merit Encyclopedia—heading "PEOPLE" within article on your country.
5. Other encyclopedias—check the articles on your country.

> NAMES OF THE PEOPLE CHOSEN:
> 1. _____
> 2. _____
> 3. _____
> 4. _____
> 5. _____

DIRECTIONS: Write a short report on each person including the information suggested below. *Remember* to make a bibliography including all references and books used on the back of this sheet.

> 1. The name of the person.
> 2. The birth place of the person.
> 3. The birth date and death date (if no longer alive).
> 4. The profession or occupation of the person.
> 5. The highlights of the person's life.
> 6. Contributions of the person.

MARCH

Lesson 1

SKILL: Practice retrieving information from the atlas.

OBJECTIVE: Students will practice locating information connected with the country chosen for project.

LITERATURE: Science fiction.

PREPARATION: A copy of "Atlas Practice Concerning _____" for each student. A transparency for introduction. Overhead projector. Prepare an introduction to science fiction. Display science fiction. Place folders on tables.

LESSON: Students take assigned seats. Check attendance. Hand out activity. Using transparency, introduce project. Students will have three lessons to complete project. Introduce science fiction. Tell briefly of books on display.

BOOK SELECTION: Students return to tables. Remind students: they must have a work of science fiction read by fourth lesson. Review lesson. Dismiss by tables. Collect folders.

Lesson 2

SKILL: Practice retrieving information from the atlas.

OBJECTIVE: Students will continue project started last week.

LITERATURE: Science fiction.

PREPARATION: Transparency of project. Overhead projector. Display science fiction. Place folders on tables.

LESSON: Students take assigned seats. Check attendance. Using transparency, review project. Students continue project. Tell briefly of books on display.

BOOK SELECTION: Students return to tables. Review progress of project. Dismiss by tables. Collect folders.

Lesson 3

SKILL: Practice retrieving information from the atlas.

OBJECTIVE: Students will complete project locating information connected with country chosen for project.

LITERATURE: Science fiction.

PREPARATION: Transparency of project. Overhead projector. Display science fiction. Place folders on tables.

LESSON: Students take assigned seats. Check attendance. Using transparency, review project. Students will complete project. Tell briefly of books on display.

BOOK SELECTION: Students return to tables. Review and discuss results of project. Remind students to have a work of science fiction read and in hand for next week's lesson. Dismiss by tables. Collect folders.

Lesson 4

SKILL: Knowledge and understanding of book report preparation.

OBJECTIVE: Students will practice preparing for a book report.

LITERATURE: Science fiction.

PREPARATION: A copy of "Book Facts and Opinions" for each student. Transparency for introduction. Overhead projector. Display selection of science fiction. Place folders on tables.

LESSON: Students take assigned seats. Check attendance. Students must have a work of science fiction read and in hand. Hand out activity. Using transparency, complete activity with the class, helping and discussing where necessary.

BOOK SELECTION: Students return to tables. Book report sheets go with students to classroom to help in writing their book reports. Dismiss by tables. Collect folders.

Name _____   Date _____

ATLAS PRACTICE
CONCERNING _____

DIRECTIONS: Using an atlas, locate the following information.

1. In what hemisphere is the country located? _____

2. In what continent is the country located? _____

3. List all the countries that border the country. _____
   _____

4. What is the capital of the country? _____

5. Name *3* large cities in the country. _____
   _____

6. Name the largest lake in the country. _____

7. Name the most important river. _____

8. Name the important physical features of the country (mountains, deserts, swamps, and the like). _____
   _____

Write the author, title, publisher, and copyright date of the atlas.

_____

_____

Draw or trace a map of the country on the back of this sheet.

A. Locate and label the following:
    1. Capital city   3. Important physical features.
    2. Three large cities   4. All countries that border the country.

APRIL

Lesson 1

SKILL: Practice retrieving information from the *Readers' Guide*.

OBJECTIVE: Students will locate at least five articles in the *Readers' Guide* concerning their project country.

LITERATURE: Adventure and sports fiction and nonfiction.

PREPARATION: *Readers' Guide.* A copy of "Magazine Articles Concerning _____" for each student. A transparency for introduction. Overhead projector. Prepare an introduction to genre. Display books in genre. Place folders on tables.

LESSON: Students take assigned seats. Check attendance. Hand out project sheets. Using transparency, introduce project. Students will need to check many issues of *Readers' Guide*. Students will have three lessons to complete project. Have students begin project. Introduce genre. Tell briefly of books on display.

BOOK SELECTION: Students return to tables. Review project. Remind students to have a work of adventure or sports fiction read by the fourth lesson. Dismiss by tables. Collect folders.

Lesson 2

SKILL: Practice retrieving information from the *Readers' Guide*.

OBJECTIVE: Students will continue project.

LITERATURE: Adventure and sports fiction and nonfiction.

PREPARATION: *Readers' Guide.* Transparency of project. Overhead projector. Display books in genre. Place folders on tables.

LESSON: Students take assigned seats. Check attendance. Using transparency, review project. Have students continue project. Tell briefly of books on display.

BOOK SELECTION: Students return to tables. Review project. Dismiss by tables. Collect folders.

Lesson 3

SKILL: Practice retrieving information from the *Readers' Guide*.

OBJECTIVE: Students will complete project.

LITERATURE: Adventure and sports fiction and nonfiction.

PREPARATION: Readers' Guide. Transparency of project. Overhead projector. Display books in genre. Place folders on tables.

LESSON: Students take assigned seats. Check attendance. Using transparency, review project. Students will complete project. Tell briefly of books on display. Place folders on tables.

BOOK SELECTION: Students return to tables. Review results of project. Remind students to have a work of adventure or sports fiction read and in hand for next lesson. Dismiss by tables. Collect folders.

Lesson 4

SKILL: Knowledge and understanding of book report preparation.

OBJECTIVE: Students will practice preparing for a book report.

LITERATURE: Adventure and sports fiction and nonfiction.

PREPARATION: A copy of *"Book Facts and Opinions"* for each student. Transparency for introduction. Overhead projector. Display selection of books in genre. Place folders on tables.

LESSON: Students take assigned seats. Check attendance. Students must have a work of adventure or sports fiction read and in hand. Using transparency, complete activity with class, helping and discussing where necessary. Tell briefly of books on display.

BOOK SELECTION: Students return to tables. Book report sheets go with students to classroom to help in writing their book reports. Dismiss by tables. Collect folders.

Name _____   Date _____

MAGAZINE ARTICLES CONCERNING _____

DIRECTIONS: 1. Using the *Readers' Guide,* locate *5* articles concerning any aspect of your country or its people.

2. If your library subscribes to the magazines, locate the articles and skim them. Determine how the articles would be of help in writing a report on the country.

List the articles below, using proper bibliographic format.

EXAMPLE: Author. "Title of article." *Title of magazine.* Volume, Number, Date of issue, Page numbers.

1. _____

_____

2. _____

_____

3. _____

_____

4. _____

_____

5. _____

_____

MAY

Lesson 1

SKILL: Knowledge and understanding of compiling a bibliography.

OBJECTIVE: Students will begin to compile a bibliography comprised of the sources used to gather information concerning their project country.

LITERATURE: Realistic problem-solving fiction and nonfiction.

PREPARATION: A copy of "A Bibliography of Materials Concerning _____," for each student. A transparency for introduction. Overhead projector. Lined paper for each student. Prepare an introduction to genre. Display books in genre. Place folders on tables.

LESSON: Students take assigned seats. Check attendance. Hand out activity sheets. Have students gather bibliographic information from folders. Using transparency, introduce activity. Have students begin activity. Introduce genre. Tell briefly of books on display.

BOOK SELECTION: Students return to tables. Review lesson. Dismiss by tables. Collect folders.

Lesson 2

SKILL: Knowledge and understanding of how to compile a bibliography.

OBJECTIVE: Students will continue to compile a bibliography of sources concerning the country of their choice.

LITERATURE: Realistic problem-solving fiction and nonfiction.

PREPARATION: Transparency of activity. Overhead projector. Lined paper for students. Display books in genre. Place folders on tables.

LESSON: Students take assigned seats. Check attendance. Using transparency, review activity. Have students continue bibliography. Students will alphabetize bibliography next week. Tell briefly of books on display.

BOOK SELECTION: Students return to tables. Review lesson. Dismiss by tables. Collect folders.

Lesson 3

SKILL: Knowledge and understanding of how to compile a bibliography.

OBJECTIVE: Students will complete the bibliography comprised of sources concerning their project country.

LITERATURE: Realistic problem-solving fiction and nonfiction.

PREPARATION: Transparency of activity. Overhead projector. Lined paper for students. Display books in genre. Place folders on tables.

LESSON: Students take assigned seats. Check attendance. Using transparency, review project. On a fresh sheet of paper, have students alphabetize bibliographies. Tell briefly of books on display.

BOOK SELECTION: Students return to tables. Review project. Remind students: they must have a work of realistic problem-solving fiction read and in hand for next week's lesson. Dismiss by tables. Collect folders.

Lesson 4

SKILL: Knowledge and understanding of book report preparation.

OBJECTIVE: Students will practice preparing for a book report.

LITERATURE: Realistic problem-solving fiction and nonfiction.

PREPARATION: A copy of "Book Facts and Opinions" for each student. A transparency for introduction. Overhead projector. Display books in genre. Place folders on tables.

LESSON: Students take assigned seats. Check attendance. Hand out activity. Students must have a work of realistic problem-solving fiction read and in hand. Using transparency, complete activity with class, helping and discussing where necessary. Tell briefly of books on display.

BOOK SELECTION: Students return to tables. Book report sheets go with students to classroom to help with writing their book reports. Dismiss by tables. Collect folders.

Name _____   Date _____

BIBLIOGRAPHY
OF MATERIALS
CONCERNING _____

DIRECTIONS: 1. Make a list of the materials used to gather information on your project country. Be sure to include all sources.
2. On a separate sheet of lined paper, write the heading BIBLIOGRA-PHY. Alphabetize the list into a bibliography.

_____

_____

_____

_____

_____

_____

_____

_____

_____

_____

_____

_____

_____

JUNE

Lesson 1

SKILL: Practice in retrieving information from reference sources.

OBJECTIVE: Students will become familiar with Greek Mythology through practice retrieving information from reference sources.

LITERATURE: Humorous fiction and nonfiction.

PREPARATION: Prepare an introduction to Greek Mythology. A copy of "Gods and Goddesses in Greek Mythology" for each student. A transparency for introduction. Overhead projector. Reference tools. Prepare an introduction to genre. Display books in genre.

LESSON: Students take assigned seats. Check attendance. Introduce and discuss Greek Mythology. Introduce project. Students will have three lessons to complete project. Introduce genre. Tell briefly of books on display.

BOOK SELECTION: Students return to tables. Review lesson. Dismiss by tables. Collect folders.

Lesson 2

SKILL: Practice in retrieving information from reference sources.

OBJECTIVE: Students will continue the Greek Mythology project.

LITERATURE: Humorous fiction and nonfiction.

PREPARATION: Transparency of project. Overhead projector. Display genre. Place folders on tables.

LESSON: Students take assigned seats. Check attendance. Using transparency, review project. Have students continue project. Tell briefly of books on display.

BOOK SELECTION: Students return to tables. Review progress of project. Dismiss by tables. Collect folders.

Lesson 3

SKILL: Practice in retrieving information from reference sources.

OBJECTIVE: Students will complete the Greek Mythology project.

LITERATURE: Humorous fiction and nonfiction.

PREPARATION: Transparency of project. Overhead projector. Display books in genre. Place folders on tables.

LESSON: Students take assigned seats. Check attendance. Using transparency, review project. Students will complete project during this lesson. Prepare bulletin board or display project in classroom. Tell briefly of books on display.

BOOK SELECTION: Students return to tables. Review project. Dismiss by tables. Collect folders.

Lesson 4

SKILL: Retention of knowledge retrieved from a reference source.

OBJECTIVE: Students will complete an activity as review of the project.

LITERATURE: As this is the last lesson there will be no book selection.

PREPARATION: A copy of "Greek Mythology" for each student. A transparency for introduction. Overhead projector. Place folders on tables.

LESSON: Students take assigned seats. Check attendance. Hand out activity. Using transparency, introduce puzzle. Have students complete puzzle. Complete puzzle together with class. If time, have class count up number of books read as a class, using students' book record sheets. Discuss any available summer reading programs. Folders go home with students. Dismiss by tables.

Name _____   Date _____

GODS AND GODDESSES IN GREEK MYTHOLOGY

DIRECTIONS: Part 1. Look up each god and goddesses. Fill in the information on the chart.

GREEK NAME	ROMAN NAME	TITLE	SYMBOL (S)	CHARACTERISTICS
APOLLO				
APHRODITE				
ARES				
ARTEMIS				
DEMETER				
DIONYSIS				
HADES				
HEPHAESTUS				
HERA				
HERMES				
HESTIA				
POSEIDON				
ZEUS				

DIRECTIONS: Part 2. Look up Mount Olympus. On the back of this sheet write a short paragraph telling where it is, what it is, why it was chosen as the home of the gods and why they left

GREEK MYTHOLOGY

ACROSS

1. The god of the dead was _____.
7. Athena was the goddess who never _____.
8. Hermes symbols were a _____ hat, shoes, and staff.
10. Hades was known as _____ in Roman mythology.
11. Hephaestus was married to _____.
15. The mischief maker of the gods was _____.
16. Mt. Olympus was the highest mountain in _____.
18. _____ was queen of the gods.
20. Poseidon carried a three-prong spear called a _____.
22. Zeus' symbol was a _____.
23. Ares was god of _____.
24. Dionysus was god of _____.
25. Aphrodite was goddess of _____.
26. Demeter was the goddess of _____.

DOWN

2. _____ was known as Mars in Roman mythology.
3. Demeter's _____ was kidnapped by Hades.
4. Zeus was _____ of the gods.
5. Athena was goddess of _____.
6. Hera was known as _____ in Roman mythology.
9. Apollo was god of _____ and poetry.
12. The ugliest of the gods was _____.
13. Poseidon was known as _____ in Roman mythology.
14. The most beloved of the gods was _____.
16. The symbol for Dionysus was the _____.
17. Aphrodite was known as _____ in Roman mythology.
19. The god whose Greek and Roman name is the same was _____.
21. Artemis was known as _____ in Roman mythology.
22. Artemis and Apollo were _____ in Greek mythology.

ANSWER KEY

Grade 1

MIXED-UP WORDS
1. SPINE
2. COVER
3. PAGES
4. DUST JACKET

HARDWARE—SOFTWARE
1. filmstrip projector (*matched to filmstrip*)
2. record player (*matched to record*)
3. cassette player (*matched to cassette*)
4. overhead projector (*matched to transparency*)
5. computer (*matched to disk*)
6. record
7. disk
8. filmstrip
9. cassette
10. transparency

FICTION—NONFICTION
The blue books would be:

E	E	E	E	E	E	E
T	S	F	D	L	A	G	V

The red books would be:

621	910	398	789	540	636	389	568
K	M	B	G	Z	P	R	N

PUZZLING WORDS
1. BOOK
2. SPINE
3. PAGES
4. READER
5. AUTHOR
6. TITLE
7. COVER
8. ILLUSTRATOR

9. PUBLISHER
10. COPYRIGHT
11. COPYRIGHT DATE

Grade 2

BIOGRAPHY, AUTOBIOGRAPHY, OR COLLECTIVE BIOGRAPHY?
1. Collective Biography
2. Autobiography
3. Collective Biography
4. Biography
5. Biography
6. Collective Biography

Grade 3

THE BUSINESS OF BOOKS

Across	Down
4. COPYRIGHT	1. PUBLISHER
6. TITLE	2. ILLUSTRATOR
7. AUTHOR	3. CALL NUMBER
8. ILLUSTRATIONS	5. PLACE OF

WHAT PART OF THE BOOK AM I?
1. spine
2. cover
3. pages
4. dust jacket
5. dedication
6. copyright

IT'S ALL PART OF THE STORY
1. a. beginning
   b. middle
   c. end
2. main
3. supporting

4. setting
5. plot

LIBRARY TERMS

Part One

1. publisher
2. illustrator
3. copyright date
4. place of publication
5. author
6. illustrations
7. title
8. copyright

Part Two

Author: Donald J. Sobol
Title: *Encyclopedia Brown's 3rd Record Book
     of Weird and Wonderful Facts*
Illustrator: Sal Murdocca
Publisher: William Morrow and Company
Copyright Date: 1985
Place of Publication: New York

THE SECRET OF SANDWICH ISLAND

1. 3, 1, 2
2. King Oswald
3. Queen Flossie and Sir Hubert
4. Pancake Island

PARTS OF THE BOOK

1. cover
2. pages
3. spine
4. dust jacket
5. title page
6. copyright page
7. copyright date
8. dedication page

THE TABLE OF CONTENTS

1. 7
2. 74
3. Birds

4. 15
5. Mountains
6. Chapter 6, "Fruits"
7. Chapter 10, "Planets"
8. 4
9. 110

THE INDEX OF A BOOK

1. 4
2. 5
3. 2
4. 36-38
5. 63, 70-72
6. 75-77, 79
7. 34-36
8. 2
9. 31, 33
10. 2
11. dash
12. comma

GUIDE WORDS

1. Aspen, Atlas, Australia
2. Mold, Mica, Mexico, Milk, Molasses
3. Pencil, Piano, Phonograph, Pavement
4. Tortilla, Thistle, Town, Throat, Tiger

USING KEY WORDS

1. *John Chapman;* Johnny Appleseed
2. *September;* Sapphire
3. *Russell Cave;* Alabama
4. *Ursa Minor;* Little Bear
5. *Mojave Desert;* California
6. *Mountain;* Mount Everest
7. *Grasshopper;* Five
8. *Cairo;* Egypt
9. *Abraham Lincoln;* 1809

ATLAS PRACTICE

1. *Florida;* Alabama, Georgia
2. *James Bay;* Canada
3. *Great Salt Lake;* Utah

4. *Denver;* Colorado

5. *Oregon;* Washington, California, Nevada, Idaho

6. *Mexico;* Texas, New Mexico, Arizona, California

7. *Toronto;* Ontario

8. *Chicago;* Lake Michigan

CARD CATALOG PUZZLE

Across	*Down*
3. NONFICTION	1. INDEX
6. THREE	2. BIOGRAPHY
7. PAGES	4. DRAWERS
11. TITLE	5. PUBLISHER
12. ALPHABETICAL	8. CALL NUMBER
13. COPYRIGHT	9. SUBJECT
14. AUTHOR	10. FICTION

BOOK TERMS SCRAMBLE

1. AUTHOR
2. ILLUSTRATOR
3. ILLUSTRATIONS
4. TITLE
5. PUBLISHER
6. PLACE OF PUBLICATION
7. COPYRIGHT
8. COPYRIGHT DATE
9. SPINE
10. MAIN CHARACTER
11. SETTING
12. PLOT
13. BEGINNING, MIDDLE, END

A BOUQUET OF FACTS

1. France
2. Answers will vary
3. Answers will vary
4. 6,696,000 (in 1981)
5. British Columbia, Saskatchewan, Northwest territories
6. Mayflower
7. North Sea
8. Red Maple
9. Ireland
10. Chile

AUTHORS AND CHARACTERS

Bond matches with Paddington

Cleary matches with Ramona

Gramatky matches with Little Toot

Haywood matches with Eddie

Keats matches with Peter

H. A. Rey matches with Curious George

Sendak matches with Max

Steig matches with Sylvester

White matches with Charlotte

Zion matches with Harry

Grade 4

PRACTICE WITH DEWEY

1. 600		11. 700	
2. 900		12. 900	
3. 600		13. 500	
4. 300		14. 500	
5. 700		15. 400	
6. 100		16. 800	
7. 600		17. 300	
8. 500		18. 400	
9. 900		19. 100	
10. 000		20. 200	

THE CARD CATALOG CAPER

Across	*Down*
4. SAINT	1. AUTHOR
7. ALPHABETICALLY	2. MISTRESS
9. THREE	3. CALL NUMBER
11. MISTER	4. SUBJECT
12. LAST	5. DOCTOR
15. SPELLED	6. MAC
16. COPYRIGHT	8. PAGES
19. DRAWERS	10. DROPPED
	13. SEE
	14. SEE ALSO
	17. INDEX
	18. TITLE

A CARD CATALOG CAPER

Across	*Down*
4. SUBJECT	1. PUBLISHER
7. ALPHABETICAL	2. DRAWERS
10. TITLE	3. COPYRIGHT
11. SEE	4. SEE ALSO
12. AUTHOR	5. CALL NUMBER
14. NONFICTION	6. LAST
15. BIOGRAPHY	8. FICTION
	9. THREE
	11. INDEX

WORLD ALMANAC PRACTICE #1

1. Newspaper Enterprises Association, Inc.
2. Hana Umlauf (answers may vary if older almanacs are used)
3. 1868
4. November
5. front of the book
6. alphabetically
7. Answers will vary
8. Answers will vary
9. buildings, tall

WORLD ALMANAC PRACTICE #2

1. Africa
2. Sandy Koufax of the Los Angeles Dodgers
3. Athens, Greece
4. Sapphire, Diamond
5. 24 carats
6. Los Alamos, New Mexico
7. Sir John A. MacDonald

WORD ALMANAC PRACTICE #3

1. 1847
2. 10 feet, 2 inches
3. Mexico City, Mexico (7,347 feet)
4. 1953
5. 1924; Chamonix, France
6. Answers will vary
7. September 17

WORLD ALMANAC PRACTICE #4

1. Quebec
2. 1979
3. Rooster—Cockerel
   Eel—Elvert
   Kangaroo—Joey
   Swan—Cygnet
   Turkey—Pout
   Hare—Leveret
4. Santa Fe, New Mexico (6,950 feet)
5. near Lebanon, Kansas (in Smith County)
6. Greenland
7. Galveston, Texas; Key West, Florida; Mobile, Alabama; New Orleans, Louisiana

REFERENCE QUEST

1. almanac
2. card catalog
3. author books
4. atlas
5. encyclopedia
6. gazetteer
7. card catalog
8. almanac
9. author books
10. encyclopedia
11. encyclopedia
12. almanac
13. atlas
14. almanac
15. card catalog

Grade 5

PARTS OF THE BOOK

1. DEDICATION PAGE
2. FRONTISPIECE
3. TITLE PAGE
4. GLOSSARY
5. BIBLIOGRAPHY
6. DUST JACKET
7. VERSO PAGE

8. PREFACE OR FOREWORD
9. TABLE OF CONTENTS
10. SPINE
11. PAGES
12. COVER
13. INDEX
14. APPENDIX

CONCEPTS AND PARTS OF THE STORY

1. DIALOGUE
2. MAIN CHARACTER
3. ILLUSTRATIONS
4. AUTHOR
5. SETTING
6. THEME
7. TITLE
8. SUPPORTING CHARACTERS
9. BEGINNING
10. PUBLISHER
11. ACTION
12. GENRE
13. ILLUSTRATOR
14. COPYRIGHT DATE
15. MIDDLE
16. PLOT
17. END
18. DESCRIPTION

PRACTICE USING A GAZETTEER OR GEOGRAPHICAL DICTIONARY

1. a village and port on an island off northeast coast of Vancouver, British Columbia
2. two and one-half miles off the east coast of Queensland, northeast Australia
3. a pueblo of Acoma Indians on a reservation 60 miles west of Albuquerque, New Mexico
4. a city in the South Transvaal Northeast Republic of South Africa, nine miles east of Johannesburg
5. seven Greek islands located in the Ionian Sea on the west coast of Greece

CARD CATALOG REVIEW

1. a. author
   b. title
   c. subject
2. a. call number
   b. author
   c. title
   d. illustrator
   e. publisher
   f. copyright date
   g. number of pages
3. alphabetically
4. author
5. title
6. subject
7. drawers
8. last
9. upper left-hand corner
10. index
11. nonfiction
12. fiction
13. true
14. true
15. true

THE CARD CATALOG "INSIDE GUIDES"

1. Ban-Bay
2. Bet-Bor
3. Ban-Bay
4. Buo-Byz
5. Bet-Bor
6. Bet-Bor
7. Bab-Ban
8. Buo-Byz
9. Bos-Bun
10. Bos-Bun
11. Bab-Ban
12. Bos-Bun
13. Buo-Byz
14. Ban-Bay

15. Bet-Bor
16. Bos-Bun
17. Bet-Bor
18. Bet-Bor
19. Bet-Bor
20. Bos-Bun

CARD CATALOG WORDSEARCH

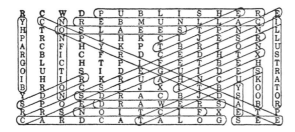

WHAT MAIN CLASS AM I?

1. 600	12. 300
2. 500	13. 800
3. 600	14. 700
4. 100	15. 600
5. 700	16. 300
6. 300	17. 900
7. 200	18. 700
8. 800	19. 900
9. 000	
10. 400	
11. 900	

FUN WITH THE ALMANAC, PART 1

1. February 8, 1910
2. Freedom of Speech, Freedom of Religion, Freedom from Want, Freedom from Fear
3. Nero
4. May 1, 1931
5. 649,739 to 1
6. April 4, 1968
7. June 24, 1848; 80,000
8. April 19, 1933
9. 3,095 miles

FUN WITH THE ALMANAC, PART 2

1. birth certificate
2. 1839-1842; Hong Kong
3. codiscoverer of insulin; 1923
4. Washington, D.C.; every day except Christmas day
5. August 20, 1920
6. 50—L
   100—C
   1,000—M
7. September 20, 1797
8. Answers may vary
9. Kroner; Peso

ABBREVIATIONS FOUND IN THE READERS' GUIDE

1. *Architectural Digest*
2. *American History Illustrated*
3. *The Bulletin of the Atomic Scientists*
4. *Creative Crafts and Miniatures*
5. *UN Monthly Chronicle*
6. annual
7. bi-monthly
8. bibliography
9. continued
10. illustrated
11. November
12. continued on later
13. July
14. August
15. October
16. publisher
17. quarterly
18. revised
19. society
20. special
21. translated
22. volume
23. year
24. March
25. June

THE READERS' GUIDE: DECODING AN ENTRY

1. CHILDREN—GROWTH AND DEVELOPMENT, E. Stark, Kids teach each other kindness., *Psychology Today, 19,* 11+, August, 1985.

2. Drake, Hokanson. *To cross America, early motorists took a long detour.,* Smithsonian, 16, 58-65, August, 1985. illustrated.

Grade 6

THE PARTS OF THE BOOK WORDSEARCH

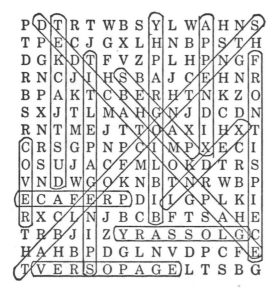

PARTS OF THE STORY WORDSEARCH

ROGET'S THEASURUS OF ENGLISH WORDS AND PHRASES

1. a. 12
   b. 0
   c. 0
   d. 12
   e. 0
   f. serious
   g. plain
2. Answers will vary

PRACTICE WITH BARTLETT'S

1. Author—Henry Wadsworth Longfellow
   Title of work—Paul Revere's Ride
   Title of book—Tales of a Wayside Inn
2. Author—George Orwell
   Title of book—Animal Farm
3. Author—Samuel Clemens (Mark Twain)
   Where, when, and to whom—in a speech to the Young People's Society, Greenpoint Presbyterian on February 16, 1901
4. Author—Herman Melville
   Title of book—Moby Dick (chapter 10)

THE FESTIVAL CALLED CHRISTMAS

1. Christianity
2. religion
3. Roman Empire
4. Christmas
5. Europe
6. European
7. Christmas
8. Christ
9. Christmas
10. British Isles
11. Christmas
12. Christmas
13. television
14. Ireland
15. Christmas
16. Scandinavian
17. Mexico

18. Spanish
19. days
20. Christmas
21. days
22. Mary
23. Joseph
24. Christ
25. candy
26. Christian
27. Christmas

THE FESTIVAL CALLED HANUKKAH

1. Hanukkah
2. Jewish
3. Lights
4. Hanukkah
5. Judaism
6. Jews
7. army
8. Temple
9. God
10. Judea
11. Greek
12. religion
13. Jews
14. army
15. army
16. Temple
17. legend
18. oil
19. light
20. oil
21. light
22. God
23. freedom of worship

GODS AND GODDESSES IN GREEK MYTHOLOGY

Aphrodite—Venus—Goddess of Love—
Dove,Sparrow,Swan,Myrtle—Beauty

Apollo—Apollo—God of Light,Music—
Lyre,Laurel

Ares—Mars—God of War—Vulture,Dog—
Fierce,Bloody

Artemis—Diana—Goddess of the Hunt—
Stag,Moon,Cypress—Cruelty

Athena—Minerva—Goddess of Wisdom—
Owl,Shield,Olive Branch—Intellectual,Wise

Demeter—Ceres—Goddess of the Harvest—
Corn—Maternal Love and Anger

Dionysus—Baccus—God of Wine—Grapes—
Violent Behavior

Hades—Pluto—God of the Under World—
Helmet,Metals,Jewels—Invisible,Gloomy

Hephaestus—Vulcan—God of Fire—
Fire,Blacksmith's Hammer—Ugly,Deformed

Hera—Juno—Queen of the Gods—
Peacock,Crow—Beauty,Jealousy

Hermes—Mercury—Messenger of the Gods—
Wand,Winged sandals and Helmet—
Graceful,Clever,Quick

Hestia—Vesta—Goddess of the Hearth—
Fire—Sweet,Gentle,Generous

Poseidon—Neptune—God of the Sea—
Trident,Horse,Bull—Stern,Restless

Zeus—Jupiter—King of the Gods—Eagle,
Shield,Thunderbolt,Oak Tree—Majestic

GREEK MYTHOLOGY

Across	*Down*
1. HADES	2. ARES
7. MARRIED	3. DAUGHTER
8. WINGED	4. KING
10. PLUTO	5. WISDOM
11. APHRODITE	6. JUNO
15. HERMES	9. MUSIC
16. GREECE	12. HEPHAESTUS
18. HERA	13. NEPTUNE
20. TRIDENT	14. HESTIA
22. THUNDERBOLT	16. GOAT
23. WAR	17. VENUS
24. WINE	19. APOLLO
25. LOVE	21. DIANA
26. HARVEST	22. TWINS